Of Time and Place:
A Shifflett-Morris Saga

A Family History
by
Anne Shifflet

©2002 by Anne Frysinger Shifflet, Ph.D.
All rights reserved
3rd edition, paperback 2017

Contents

Contents iii
List of Illustrations v
Preface vii
    Abbreviations viii
    Numbers viii
    Acknowledgments viii
    Dedication ix
Chapter 1: A Point in Time 1
Chapter 2: From the Mattaponi to the Mountains 11
Chapter 3: Cousins on the County Line 27
Chapter 4: A Farm on Flat Gut Run 41
Chapter 5: Between the Blue Ridge and Huckleberry Mountain 67
Chapter 6: What Happened to Kennel? 79
Chapter 7: On Top of the Mountain 97
Chapter 8: Ambrose and the Exodus 115
Chapter 9: A Place Remembered 133
Appendix A: Family Records 137
Ancestors of Ambrose Washington Shifflett 139
Ancestors of Laura Belle Morris 141
Children of Ambrose W. and Laura (Morris) Shifflett 143
Appendix B: Records of the Shenandoah National Park 147
Bibliography of Published Sources 155
Index of Names 161

List of Illustrations

Ambrose Washington Shifflett and Laura Belle (Morris) Shifflett ix
The Pamunkey River 13
The Cohoke Swamp 17
The Mattaponi River at Courthouse Landing 19
The Mattaponi River 21
The Blue Ridge Mountains 21
Map of County Seats 22
Map of current county boundaries 25
Map of the Orange/Albemarle County Line 29
Bacon Hollow from the Skyline Drive Overlook 43
Map of Flat Gut Run to Orange and Stanardsville 46
Bacon Hollow and Flat Top Mountain 53
Burton Morris and Samantha (Frazier) Morris 57
"Bev" Morris 62
Sarah Catherine Morris 62
Mary Frances and Daniel Morris 62
Cecelia "Cissie" Morris 64
Laura Belle Morris 65
Marriage Bond of John Lawson and Eva Harnist 68
Map of Hawksbill Creek area 70
Gravestones of John and Eva Lawson 71
Huckleberry Mountain 73
Eve Shifflett about 1870 91
Gravestone of Eve Shifflett 93
William J. Shifflett 94

Ambrose W. Shifflett	94
Jonas Shifflett	95
Alice and Melvin Hansbrough	95
Roadside School in Beldor Hollow	99
Map of Shifflett-Morris locations on the Blue Ridge	100
Road to Simmons Gap	106
Tools for repairing shoes and darning socks	107
Laura Morris Shifflett's spinning wheel	108
Ambrose Shifflett's mountain-top home and garden	109
Kenneth Shifflet as a toddler	110
Children on the front porch	110
Children near the barn	110
Neighbors visit at the Simmons Gap Episcopal mission church	111
Kenneth outside the Simmons Gap Episcopal mission church	112
Straight razor, shaving brush and mug	112
Family photo near Simmons Gap	113
Ambrose and Laura's farm in Pennsylvania	128
Ambrose with his three mules	129
50th wedding anniversary	130
Family and friends boil applebutter	131
Tombstone in Hanoverdale, Pennsylvania	131
Chimney of the demolished home	133
Retaining wall near the old home	134
The timeless mountains of the Blue Ridge	135
Plat of Rockingham County, Tract #178	150
Plat of Rockingham County, Tract #180	151

Preface

Who we are and what we become is largely dependent upon the time and place that we are born. The genetic heritage from our parents is important. The particular circumstances of our immediate environment are influential. But these are cradled in the era, the history, and the assumptions of people living in a given setting. We all are a product of time and place.

It is from this perspective that I have written this saga—a story in which events of 250 years are chronicled. I have drawn from the works of prominent historians to set the stage on which the Shifflett and Morris ancestors are the key players. As we attempt to understand their activities and decisions, it can be helpful to imagine ourselves in their time and place.

Many of you may read this as a genealogy. The paucity of early Virginia records makes a well-documented genealogy impossible. There is no black book where births of children are recorded with correct birthdates and names of parents! We are fortunate that many, but not all, marriages were recorded. Some even mention the stated age and the parents of bride and groom. Land records often provide useful clues to relationships.

On the other hand, census records are obviously full of inconsistencies. Even 20th century death certificates and tombstones are only as accurate as the information provided after the fact by children, in-laws, or neighbors. Think about it. How many of your neighbors—or sons-in-law—know the names of your parents and the exact day you were born? We rely on written notes to aid our faulty memories. The majority of our ancestors who could not read or write did not have that advantage.

When compiling lists of children of a given couple, I have based my best guess on available records. In each case I have identified the source of my information. There is always the possibility of attaching the information to another person with the same name. I apologize for the inevitable errors.

Spelling was not standardized until relatively recently. The clerk of court wrote names as he heard them. Occasionally Morris was written with an extra "s." And, fussy as we may be about getting the right number of "f"s and "t"s in our Shiflet, Shiflett, Shifflet or Shifflett, there is no "correct" way to spell the surname!

Anne F. Shifflet

Abbreviations

I have tried to avoid abbreviations, other than the customary ones for state names, e.g., Va. and Md. However, in the source notes, the following are used:

aka	also known as	m.	married
b.	born	p.	page
c.	circa (about)	pp.	pages
Co.	County	pr.	proved or probated
d.	died	s/o	son of
d/o	daughter of		

In handwritten original documents, many words are illegible. In some of the quoted portions, I have attempted to copy the letters as they appear, even when the spelling doesn't make sense. A question mark in brackets is attached, e.g., "ancs[?]." A separate [?] indicates a complete illegible word.

Numbers

A pedigree (Ahnentafel) numbering system is used in this book with numbers of direct ancestors placed in square brackets after their names. Each father's number is twice that of his child; the mother's number is twice plus one (e.g., Burton Morris [6], his father, Jeremiah Morris [12], and his mother, Peachy Shiflett [13]). Maiden names are used throughout.

The numbers are specific to the direct ancestors of Ambrose Shifflett and Laura Morris and correlate with the pedigrees in Appendix A. However, within each chapter, the numbers clarify relationships and can help keep the generations in perspective.

Acknowledgments

Many persons have generously shared their memories of life on the Blue Ridge. I am grateful to Elizabeth Meadows, Barbara Shifflett Hensley, Larry F. Shifflett, Victoria Baugher Hensley, Casey Billhimer, Norman Addington, Eugene Powell, Dale MacCalister, Martin Walter, the Alderman Library at the University of Virginia, the Menno Simons Historical Library at Eastern Mennonite University, the Bridgewater College library, and family members, Beulah Shifflett Herring, Otto Shifflet, Edna Shiflet Parrell, and Gordon Boardway, for sharing documents and photographs. Allen Shifflet's thoughtful review of the manuscript was greatly appreciated.

Dedicated to my husband, Kenneth E. Shifflet,
and to the memory of his parents,
Ambrose W. Shifflett and Laura B. (Morris) Shifflett,
whose triumphs over great odds
inspired the recapture of this family history.

Ambrose Washington Shifflett and Laura Belle (Morris) Shifflett

1 A Point in Time

Raising tobacco was hard work. Clearing a patch of land in the forest by felling or girdling the trees was just the beginning. There was seasonal work requiring all four seasons, with no vacation from toil under the hot sun of Virginia summers or the wet winds of winter.

In February, the tobacco seeds were sown in beds that had been prepared, "hoed up again, raked, laid off."[1] During March and April, the fields were prepared for transplanting the seedlings. The soil was hoed up into "hills" about three feet apart. Old fields were fertilized with dung dug up from the cattle pens, dried, and carried to the fields. A vigilant eye was kept on the young tobacco plants during the unpredictable spring weather. They were covered and uncovered with bundles of brush to protect them from frost.

In order to ensure the necessary water for transplanting the seedlings, rainy days in May prompted a rush to the fields. Each of the tobacco seedlings was set into a prepared hill, and each field hand was expected to transplant a thousand seedlings a day.[2]

Throughout the summer, they weeded the tobacco and picked off the worms. They broke off the "suckers," branches which developed in the axils of the leaf. Sometimes they removed the flower head so that leaves at the bottom of the plant would develop more fully. In September they began cutting stalks with six to eight leaves. The withered stalks were put on pointed sticks and hung in a tobacco house to dry. The winter task of stripping tobacco began in late October. The dried stalks were shaken down and covered up in bulk to sweat, then leaves were pulled from the stems and tied up in bundles.

These "hands" of tobacco were packed in a boat, in a cart, or in a wooden "hogshead" to be rolled to the warehouse on a "rowling road."[3] At the public warehouse, an official inspector would certify the tobacco as "merchantable" or, sometimes, order it burned as trash. Meanwhile, on the plantation other men were already at work preparing new fields for the crude hoes which would be used to break the sod for another growing season.

---

[1] Rhys Isaac, *The Transformation of Virginia, 1740–1790* (New York: W. W. Norton, 1982), pp. 23-27. The seasonable tasks are described in entries in a 1766 diary of plantation owner Landon Carter who lived on the northern side of the Rappahannock River.
[2] Isaac, *Transformation*, p. 24.
[3] A hogshead was a wooden cask generally 4' high and 2½ feet in diameter.

As with any agricultural product, success and profit in raising tobacco were subject to both the vagaries of the weather and the uncertainties of price. Yet nearly everyone in colonial Virginia was involved with raising tobacco.

It was not planned that way. Virginia was to have been the colony that could provide raw materials and products to mitigate England's economic woes.

During the 16th century, it was the superiority of Spanish ships and the expertise of Spanish sailors and navigators that enabled exploration of the American coast. Christopher Columbus came upon the islands of the West Indies in 1492, and the search was on for the "western passage" that would allow ships to easily reach the known riches of Cathay. Just five years after Columbus' discovery, merchants of Bristol, England, sent out John Cabot (really the Spaniard, Giovanni Caboto) to find a northern route to Cathay. He discovered Cape Breton, Newfoundland, and Labrador and claimed these areas for the English.

Spaniards made voyages to South America and Ponce de Leon came as far north as Florida in 1513. However, the eastern coast of what became the United States remained uncharted. From 1534–1541, the French explorer, Jacques Cartier, explored the St. Lawrence River and established the French presence in Canada. In 1565, the Spanish built the first town in America, St. Augustine, and sent missionaries as far north as the Chesapeake Bay.

Queen Elizabeth silently encouraged the English privateers who, while seeking and destroying Spanish treasure ships, scouted the southeastern coastline. The entire area from present Florida to Maine was referred to as "Virginia" in honor of the Virgin Queen. A favorite courtier of Elizabeth was the poet, historian, and adventurer, Sir Walter Raleigh. During the 1580's, Raleigh established the ill-fated Roanoke Island colony where all the settlers perished. The continuing war for supremacy of the seas discouraged all efforts at discovery along the Atlantic seaboard for a generation.

In 1600, there was not a single English or Frenchman in America.[4] English statesmen knew that survival of their country depended upon colonial expansion. Many of England's forests had been long depleted. Over the years, the development of agriculture had demanded open fields and the wood was used for fuel and houses. But in 1600, three major English industries required timber. It was essential to build ships for the importing and exporting of salt, sugar, spices, silk, dyes, and fruit. Manufacture of woolens required potash, and charcoal was needed for the smelting of iron.

---

4 "Discovery and Exploration of America," *Encyclopedia Americana* (New York: Americana Corporation, 1960), 1, pp. 489-491.

Not only had the early explorers reported unending forests along the Virginia coastline, there was an urgency to establish a foothold in the New World before Spain got it all. England needed to break its economic dependence on European competitors.[5]

The Virginia Company of London was organized in 1606 for the purpose of founding an English colony on the North American seacoast. It was granted a royal charter to establish a settlement and exploit the resources of any area located between 34° and 41° north latitude. The Company was comprised of two groups of men: "Adventurers" who stayed in England and subscribed money towards capital stock, and "Planters" who went in person to plant a colony in Virginia.[6]

On 13 May 1607, on a marshy peninsula 32 miles from the mouth of the James River, the colony of Jamestown was founded by the Virginia Company These earliest settlers were not looking for new homes. They sought to establish a "plantation" of temporary residents to undertake a commercial enterprise. All decision making power was vested in a council located in London. The planters were promised money and 500 acres of land after seven years.[7]

The Company didn't hesitate to begin exploitation of available resources. In 1608, they imported some Dutchmen and Poles to help start up pitch, tar, turpentine and potash manufactures.[8] However, the imposed restrictions on planting corn caused chronic food shortages.[9] During the winter of 1609–1610, Jamestown was almost wiped out by famine. The remaining settlers had abandoned the colony and were already on a ship expecting to return to England when Thomas West, Baron De La Warr (Lord Delaware) arrived on 7 Jun 1610 with supplies and additional colonists.[10]

The village was reoccupied and new industries were attempted. There was an abundance of timber to burn to manufacture potash.[11] There was plenty of iron ore and an ambitious, expensive smelting plant was built. However, before it reached full production, it was destroyed by Indians in 1622.

All of these industrial attempts failed because of the lack of cheap labor. New arrivals in Jamestown were particularly susceptible to the deadly summer diseases of

---

[5] Thomas J. Wertenbaker, *The Planters of Colonial Virginia* (1922, reprint, Baltimore: Genealogical Publishing Co., 1997), pp. 7-14.
[6] James Curtis Ballagh, *White Servitude in the Colony of Virginia* (Baltimore: John Hopkins University Studies, 13th Series, No. VI-VII, 1895), p. 11.
[7] Ballagh, *White Servitude in the Colony of Virginia,* p. 16.
[8] Wertenbaker, *Planters of Colonial Virginia*, pp. 15, 18.
[9] Ballagh, *White Servitude in the Colony of Virginia,* p. 14.
[10] "Jamestown," *Encyclopedia Americana* (1960), 15, p. 609.
[11] The ashes from 2½ to five acres of well-timbered land were required to make a ton of crude pearlash. From wood-ashes, potassium salts could be recovered and used for making soap, dyes, and glass. "Potash," *Encyclopedia Americana* (1960), 22, p. 440.

typhoid, malaria, and amoebic dysentery. The few remaining workers commanded pay of up to five times the going rate in England. The cost of the long ocean journey made it impossible to transport enough of England's unemployed to Virginia.

Only one enterprise proved successful. John Rolfe, the husband of Pocahontas, had smoked and tasted the leaf the Indians savored. Rolfe experimented with the plant and improved the flavor of the tobacco leaf. He sent samples of the tobacco to England, where it was proclaimed to have excellent quality. Smoking had become a stylishly strong custom in England and the Virginia leaf was superior to the Spanish product for which England was paying thousands of pounds! The Virginia colonists immediately turned to planting tobacco in every cleared patch of land. In 1617, 20,000 pounds were exported on the first shipload to England. Ten years later, about 500,000 pounds were exported.[12]

To the dismay of the British who had hoped for an industrial colony to supply the needs of the mother country, and to the Virginia Company who had hoped to grow rich in the process,[13] Virginia had become an agricultural society based on one commodity.

> March 1629/30. "To prevent the want of corne which oftentymes doth happen to this colony by reason of the neglect of planting sufficient quantities thereof for their necessarie provisions, It is ordered, that two acres of corne or neere thereabouts bee planted for every head that worketh in the grounds, and the same to bee sufficiently tended weeded and preserved from birdes, hoggs, cattell and other inconveniences. And if any planter shall bee found delinquent therein hee shall forfeite all his tobaccoe which bee made of his cropp that yeare, the one halfe, to the informer, the other to bee imployed to publique uses for the good of the country . . ."
>
> "For the improving the planting of tobaccoe the neglect thereof in the curing hath caused the same to bee of base price and small esteem to the discredit and disadvantage of the whole colony in generall, for the preventing and avoyding whereof, *It is thought fitt and accordingly ordered*, That noe person whatsoever shall plant or tende above two thousand plants of tobaccoe for every heade within his family including weoman and children."
>
> February 1632/33. "*Be it further ordered*, That no planter or master of a familie, shall plant or cause to be planted above 1500 plants per pol. . ."
>
> William Walker Hening, *The Statutes at Large; being A Collection of all the Laws of Virginia, from the First Session of the Legislature, in the Year 1619*, volume 1 (Richmond, 1809), pp. 152, 205.

---

12 Wertenbacher, *Planters in Colonial Virginia*, pp. 24-25. Information from G. L. Beer, *The Origins of the British Colonial System*, p. 79.

13 The King was dissatisfied and the Virginia Company charter was annulled. In 1624, Virginia became a royal colony.

But the need for affordable labor had not diminished. The leaders of the fledgling colony had to figure out a method for bringing unemployed men and women from England to work in the tobacco fields.

A scheme for importing "indentured servants" was soon in practice and was formalized into law in 1619.[14] It was a simple plan. Any person over the age of fifteen could bind himself over to a shipping merchant who, in return for giving him a free passage to America, could sell him to the highest bidder for servitude in the plantations. A strict contract (indenture) ensured the obligation to work for a specified time to earn their passage money. Severe penalties were proscribed for any breaches of contract. But at the end of their term, usually five to seven years, the workers were free.

The scheme provided an opportunity for idle or adventurous English youth to search for new prospects in life; most of the indentured servants were from 17 to 23 years old when they arrived in America. It gave English authorities the opportunity to clear the jails of petty criminals—deportation was often more merciful than the harsh penalties of the time. And the plan created a profitable business for recruiters. Seventeenth century Bristol merchants had few scruples about how they obtained their recruits. An unskilled man could be sold for £10, a skilled craftsman for £25. At that time, transatlantic passenger fare was about £4.[15]

In Virginia, the number of indentured servants was sharply increased by the "headright" system enacted by the Virginia Company in 1618. Under it, each person who was willing to pay for his own passage and settle in Virginia was offered fifty acres of land. Furthermore, he was entitled to an additional fifty acres for each member of his family and for each servant that he brought along.[16] The practice continued after Virginia became a royal colony in 1624 and remained a major incentive for immigration. Throughout the 1600s, about 2000 immigrants were recorded every year.[17]

As long as land was plentiful and the price of tobacco was high, it was not too difficult for indentured persons who had completed their terms of servitude to become independent. They could work for wages for a few years, then buy a place of their own. Although the best river-front lands had been usurped by the wealthy plantation owners, there were lesser tracts available on the higher "necks" between the rivers at a fraction of the cost. A man could raise tobacco as profitably on a small tract as on a large plantation.

---

14 Virginius Dabney, *Virginia: The New Dominion* (New York: Doubleday, 1971), p. 29.
15 Peter Wilson Coldham, *Bonded Passengers to America: Vol.1, History of Transportation, 1615–1775* (Baltimore: Genealogical Publishing Company, 1983), p. 7.
16 "Headrights," Online VA Notes from The Library of Virginia, downloaded 23 Aug 1999. Intended to promote settlement and ownership of small farms, the program was subject to abuse and fraud. A small number of merchants, shippers, and speculators accumulated large tracts of land. See also the introduction to volume one of Nell M. Nugent, *Cavaliers and Pioneers* (Richmond, 1979).
17 Wertenbaker, *Planters in Colonial Virginia*, p. 35.

October, 1705.

"And also be it enacted, by the authority aforesaid, and it is hereby enacted, That all masters and owner of servants, shall find and provide for their servants, wholesome and competent diet, clothing, and lodging, by the discretion of the county court; and shall not, at any time, give immoderate correction; neither shall, at any time, whip a christian white servant naked, without an order from a justice of peace . . ."

"And be it also enacted, by the authority aforesaid, and it is hereby enacted, That if any minister or reader shall wittingly publish, or suffer to be published, the banns of matrimony, between any servants, or between any free person and a servant; or if a minister shall wittingly celebrate the rites of matrimony between any such, without a certificate from the master or mistress of every such servant, that it is done by their onsent, he shall forfeit and pay ten thousand pounds of tobacco: And every servant so married, without the consent of his or her master or mistress, shall, for his or her said offence, serve his or her master or mistress, their executors, administrators, or assigns, one whole year, after the time of service, by indenture or custom, is expired: And moreover, every person being free and so marrying with a servant, shall, for his or her said offence, forfeit and pay to the master or owner of such servant, one thousand pounds of tobacco, or well and faithfully serve the said master or owner of the said servant one whole year, in actual service."

"And if any women servant shall be delivered of a bastard child within the time of her service aforesaid, Be it enacted, by the authority aforesaid, and it is to be thereby enacted, That in recompence of the loss and trouble occasioned her master or mistress thereby, she shall for every such offence, serve her said master or owner one whole year after her time by indenture, custom, and former order of court, shall be expired; or pay her said master or owner, one thousand pounds of tobacco; and the reputed father, if free, shall give security to the church wardens of the parish where that child may be, to maintain the child, and keep the parish indemnified; or be compelled thereto by order of the county court, upon the said church-wardens complaints: But if a servant, he shall make satisfaction to the parish, for keeping the said child, after his time by indenture, custom, or order of court, to his then present master or owner, shall be expired; or be compelled thereto, by order of the county court, upon complaint of the church-wardens of the said parish, for the time being.

"And if any woman servant shall be got with child by her master, neither the said master, nor his executors, administrators, nor assigns shall have any claim of service against her, for or by reason of such child; but she shall, when her time due to her said master, by indenture, custom or order of court, shall be expired, be sold by the churchwardens, for the time being, of the parish wherein such child shall be born, for one year, or pay one thousand pounds of tobacco; and the said one thousand pounds of tobacco, or whatever she shall be sold for, shall be emploied, by the vestry, to the use of the said parish."

But the early high prices of tobacco declined. The Virginia supply became greater than the English demand. At first, the surplus was sold for a good price to eager Dutch and other European customers. But a Navigation Act passed by England in 1651 reinforced the rule that the colonies were permitted to trade commodities such as tobacco only with the mother country, and in English ships. England would then re-export some of the raw product to Europe. A second Navigation Act enacted in 1661 was designed to further ensure the balance of British exports over British imports. The King essentially told complaining Virginians that the only solution to their predicament was to produce other raw products that were needed in England. With the cost of clothing and farm implements imported to Virginia remaining high, the profit for many colonial tobacco producers disappeared.[18]

Another, even more powerful force was changing the economy of Virginia—the growing prevalence of slavery. The first black Africans arrived in Jamestown in 1619 aboard a Dutch ship. They were probably sold as indentured servants. But as more blacks were gradually brought into the colony, they were sold to the wealthier planters as slaves. The General Assembly legalized Negro slavery in 1661. Ten years later,

> " . . . be it enacted, and declared, That in all cases of penal laws, wherby persons free are punishable by fine, servants shall be punished by whipping, after the rate of twenty lashes for every five hundred pounds of tobacco, or fifty shillings current money, unless the servant so culpable, can and will procure some person or persons to pay the fine."
>
> ". . . and it is hereby enacted, That all servants (not being slaves), whether imported, or become servants of their own accord here, or bound by any court or churchwardens, shall have their complaints received by a justice of the peace, who, if he find cause, shall bind the master over to answer the complaint at court; and it shall be there determined . . . upon a second just complaint, [the court] to order such servant to be immediately sold at an outcry, by the sheriff, and after charges deducted, the remainder of what the said servant shall be sold for, to be paid and satisfied to such owner."
>
> ". . . it is hereby enacted, That there shall be paid and allowed to every imported servant, not having yearly wages, at the time of service ended, by the master or owner of such servant, viz: To every male servant, ten bushels of indian corn, thirty shillings in money, or the value thereof in goods, and one well fixed musket or fuzee, of the value of twenty shillings, at least, and to every woman servant, fifteen bushels of indian corn, and forty shillings in money, or the value thereof in goods."
>
> William Walter Hening, *The Statutes at Large: being a Collection of all the Laws of Virginia*, 13 volumes (1823, reprint, Charlottesville, Va.: University Press of Virginia, 1969), 3, pp. 444-453.

---

18 Wertenbaker, *Planters in Colonial Virginia*, pp. 68-71.

Virginia's Governor Berkley reported that of the total 40,000 population of Virginia, 6,000 were white indentured servants and 2,000 were Negro slaves.[19]

The planters with larger acreage were discovering that the cost of maintaining an adequate work force of indentured servants was prohibitively high. When the servant's terms were completed after just a few years, they were free to go. Replacements had to be procured and trained. Some estate inventory records indicate that the price of a sturdy man servant varied from £2 to £4 for each year of his service. A planter could buy a slave for £18 to £20. The slave served for life, and so did his children.[20]

Slavery brought prosperity to the large planters, but spelled ruin for the farmer who worked with his own hands. Many small planters who could not compete sold out to wealthier neighbors and emigrated to other colonies. Some who could buy one or a few slaves were able to hold on. The freeholders without servants or slaves did not completely disappear, but gradually declined in number and many sank into abject poverty.

Fewer newly freed indentured servants could establish their own farms. It was difficult to secure any land in Tidewater Virginia because of the large tracts patented[21] by rich planters. The margin of profit that had allowed freedmen to advance rapidly had been wiped out during the depression of tobacco prices. The indentured servant who came over after 1660 found conditions in the colony hardly more favorable for his advancement than in England.[22]

As both the need and opportunities for indentured servants diminished, so did the number of those transported. The stream of about 2,000 a year had remained remarkably constant through the 1600s. Now, at the beginning of the 18th century, the flow of white servants from the mother country almost stopped. In 1702, there were about 1,000; in 1715, only 91 indentured servants arrived in Virginia.[23]

---

19 Virginius Dabney, Virginia: *The New Dominion* (New York: Doubleday, 1971), pp. 51-53.
20 Wertenbaker, *Planters in Colonial Virginia*, p. 127.
21 In Colonial Virginia, ownership of land was legally assigned to individuals through the issue of patents. The patent conveyed all rights to the land. Subsequent transfers of property were in the form of deeds.
22 Wertenbaker, *Planters in Colonial Virginia*, p. 96.
23 Wertenbaker, *Planters in Colonial Virginia*, p. 134.

> Spelling had not become standardized in the 18th century. In many colonial documents, one individual's surname may appear with several different spellings. Often spelling in official records was dependent on what the clerk heard, or thought he heard. Changes in handwriting practices also create problems for modern readers. For example, in the 1700s, the letter "s" in the middle of a word was represented by a tall, rather straight character extending both above and below the line. It is easily mistaken for an "f" and vice versa.

From 1702 to 1714, six headrights were obtained for the importation of men with surnames recorded as Siflett, Shiflett, Sislett, and Sistlett.[24] It was at this point in time that these men left England to seek their place in the colony of Virginia.

---

24 There is no evidence to prove or disprove that these spellings are variations or incorrect transcriptions of the same surname. However, lack of later records citing the "Siflet," "Sislett," and "Siflett" surnames, and the frequency of encountering the name Shiflet/Shiflett/Shifflet/Shifflett suggests that the immigrants may have been of the same surname group. That possibility must be considered.

2 From the Mattaponi to the Mountains

The Blue Ridge Mountains beyond the western horizon were the stuff of dreams for men living in Tidewater Virginia in 1700. A German scholar, John Lederer, had explored the highlands in 1670 and found that "the ground is overgrown with underwood in many places, and that so perplext and interwoven with vines, that who travels here, must sometimes cut through his way."[1] Upon reaching the top of a high mountain peak and seeing only more, even higher mountains, he concluded, "They are certainly in a great error, who imagine the continent of North-America is but eight or ten days journey over from the Atlantick to the Indian ocean . . ."[2]

However, the Virginia leaders paid little attention to Lederer's report. Over the next half century, only a few fur traders ventured into the wilderness. As the colony expanded outward from Jamestown, the settled land was divided into new counties. But the western boundaries of these counties were undefined. Many still believed that a pass might be found that would lead to the western sea.

Meanwhile, the tobacco planters were intent on enlarging their holdings and their work force. Acquiring land through the headright system was not always a straight forward, predictable transaction. The ship's captain would provide proof of the number of passages from England that an individual had paid. Headrights could be granted for oneself, or for members of one's family or friends, as well as for servants. The ship's captain or a cooperating merchant sold the servants to the highest bidder. Two copies of a contract stating the length and terms of service were written—on the same paper. The paper was then cut or torn with a jagged edge so that the matching indentures could provide proof of ownership. Sometimes these contracts were transferred to others, with the servants being bought and sold as slaves. Thus, the person who got a patent was not necessarily the one who had paid the transportation costs of the immigrant. The usual procedure was for a person entitled to a headright to take his evidence given by the

---

1 John Lederer, *The Discoveries of John Lederer*, translated by Sir William Talbot (London: Heyrick, 1672), p. 5. The Albert H. Small Special Collections Library, University of Virginia Library.
2 Lederer, *Discoveries of John Lederer*, p. 26.

> In 1716, Governor Alexander Spotswood organized an expedition to investigate the hills of the Blue Ridge. The party included at least four surveyors and "some of the canniest land speculators in all the province." Their primary purpose was to explore the western Virginia frontier, thus encouraging settlement. It also enabled the land men to turn handsome profits on huge tracts claimed for themselves. Because of a memento Spotswood gave to each of his traveling companions, they are referred to as the "Knights of the Golden Horseshoe."
>
> Edward P. Alexander, editor, *Journal of John Fontaine* (Williamsburg: Colonial Williamsburg Foundation, 1972), p. 13.

ship's captain to a county court and obtain a certificate of entitlement. Fraudulent claims were sometimes made by presenting similar evidence to more than one authority.[3]

The certificate of entitlement was taken to the office of the secretary of the colony, who issued the "headright" or right to patent fifty acres of land. The land was then surveyed by the county surveyor. After returning the survey and the headright to the secretary's office, a patent was granted for the tract of land.[4] This may have been done expediently, or the process could have been drawn out for a generation or so. The patentee might not have even known the immigrant!

Thus, the list of "transported persons" named as the basis for the issue of a patent only proves that these individuals were actually physically present in Virginia prior to the date on the patent. Nevertheless, the land descriptions in the patents can help identify the landowners' tracts and provide clues as to the locations where the indentured servants might have toiled, and other places they might have heard about.

With headright claims, George Alves (Alvis) acquired thousands of acres in New Kent County. A headright claim on 7 Nov 1700 for 767 acres in St. Peter's Parish, New Kent County, was based on the importation of 16 persons including Joseph Wyatt and John and Mary Davis.[5] The area in which Alves lived was divided out of St. Peter's and became St. Paul's Parish in 1704.[6] On 16 Dec 1714, George Alves was granted a patent for 4,843 acres of new land in St. Paul's Parish. The tract was described as "beginning at Col. James Taylor at head of Meadow Branch; to Taylor's Creek; to south branch of Pamunkey River, called the South River," and was awarded for the transportation of 97 persons including Jno. Sislett and Stephen Sislett.[7]

---

[3] James W. Doyle, Jr., "The Mayflower Comes to Virginia, 1633," *Tidewater Virginia Families*, Volume 3, No. 4, p. 210.

[4] "Headrights," Online *VA-Notes* from the Library of Virginia.

[5] Nell Marion Nugent, abstractor and indexer, *Cavaliers and Pioneers*: Volume 3:1695–1732 (Richmond: Virginia State Library, 1979), pp. 37, 39. Patent Book 9-284.

[6] Charles Frances Cocke, *Parish Lines, Diocese of Virginia* (Richmond, Va.: Virginia, 1967), p. 222.

[7] Nugent, *Cavaliers and Pioneers*, III, p. 162. Patent Book 10-212.

The Pamunkey River east of the Cohoke Swamp. A land of tobacco plantations in colonial Virginia, the rich agricultural area now produces corn, soybeans, and cotton.

When Hanover county was formed in 1721, St. Paul's Parish covered the whole new county. Alves was able to acquire more of the land.[8] He was a neighbor of another large landowner, William Morris.[9] When Fredericksville Parish was created in 1742 and covered all of the new Louisa County in 1744, they were residents there.

In 1700, King and Queen County, with 4,306 inhabitants, was the second most populous in Virginia.[10] But it lost its only town to the new King William County in 1702.

Abraham Willory of St. John's Parish in King William County was granted a patent deed for 445 acres of land on the Pamunkey Neck on 28 Oct 1702. The acreage began at the Long branch, extended "to the mouth thereof on St. John's Creek" and to the Acquinton swamp. The headright was based on the transportation of nine persons to Virginia, including one Stephen Siflet.[11]

---

8 Nugent, *Cavaliers and Pioneers,* III, pp. 247, 277, 295 and 400.
9 Nugent, *Cavaliers and Pioneers*, III, p. 260.
10 Website of King and Queen County.
11 Nugent, *Cavaliers and Pioneers*, 3, p. 62. The transaction is recorded in Patent Book 9-484.

On 26 Apr 1712, George Slaughter, also living in St. John's Parish in King William County, received a patent for 145 acres of new land adjoining his previously owned land. This was his headright based on the importation of three persons: Elizabeth Collins, John Shiflett, and Gilbert Ellett.[12] Slaughter had acquired 200 acres in St. John's Parish on the Pamunkey Neck on 24 Oct 1701.[13] This land was located at the "mouth of Slaughter's Branch, out of Cohoake Swamp on the West side." His new adjoining tract was on the "west side of Cohoke Swamp."[14]

Many of the patents granted for "new land" during the early years of the 18th century were for tracts along the Mattaponi River, which separated King William County from King and Queen County (north of Williamsburg.) The capitol had moved to Williamsburg in 1699, and this was a growing edge of the Virginia colony.

In the royal colony of Virginia, each person was deemed a member of the Church of England. Some of the first legislative acts clarified the responsibilities of attendance and uniformity to the Established Church.

March 1623–4 — 21st James, 1st.

Act 1. That in every plantation, where the people use to meete for the worship of god, a house or rooms sequestered for that purpose, and not to be for any temporal use whatsoever, and a place empaled in, sequestered only to the buryal of the dead.

Act 2. That whosoever shall absent himselfe from divine service any Sunday without an allowable excuse shall forfeite a pound of tobacco, and he that absenteth himselfe a month shall forfeit 50 lb. of tobacco.

Act 3. That there be an uniformity in our church as neere as may be to the canons in England; both in substance and circumstance, and that all persons yeild [sic]readie obedience unto them under paine of censure.[1]

---

1 William Walker Hening, *The Statutes at Large Being a Collection of all the Laws of Virginia, from the First Session of the Legislature in the Year 1619*, Volume 1 (Richmond: Printer to the Commonwealth, 1809), pp. 122-123.

---

12 Nugent, *Cavaliers and Pioneers*, III, p. 127. Patent Book 10-64.
13 Nugent, *Cavaliers and Pioneers*, III, p. 50. Patent Book 9-385.
14 The Cohoke Swamp is located in southeastern King William County, east of the Pamunkey Indian Reservation.

The Anglican worship consisted almost entirely of reading the services from the Book of Common Prayer.[1] The clergy stressed the sacredness of authority and the need for subjects to honor and revere those set over them.[2]

Because no Bishop was ever sent from England, the Church in Virginia was unable to enact its own laws. The General Assembly established parish boundaries and asserted authority over the Church. Each parish was ruled by a vestry of twelve gentlemen presided over by the minister.[3] The vestry had authority and responsibility to pay the minister's salary, to buy lands for churches, erect buildings, and to care for the poor and orphaned children. Expenses were covered by taxes or "tithes" levied on all "tithables" in the parish. Quakers and other nonconformists were not welcome in the colony.

March 1659–60.

> Act VI. An Act for the suppressing the Quakers. Whereas there is an vnreasonable and turbulent sort of people, commonly called Quakers, who contrary to the law do dayly gather together vnto them vnlaw'll Assemblies and congregations of people teaching and publishing, lies, miracles, false visions, prophecies, and doctrines . . . attempting thereby to destroy religion, laws, communities and all bonds of civil societies . . ."
>
> It is enacted, That no master or commander of any shipp or other vessell do bring into this collonie any person or persons called Quakers, under the penalty of one hundred pounds sterling to be leavied vpon him . . . That all such Quakers as have been questioned or shall hereafter arrive shall be apprehended wheresoever they shall be found and they be imprisoned without baile or mainprize till they do abjure this country or putt in security with all speed to depart the collonie and not to returne again . . .[4]

After Virginia adopted the English Edict of Toleration in April 1699, dissenters were no longer required to attend the Established Church, but attendance "at any congregation or place of religious worship permitted and allowed by the said act of Parliament"[5] was mandatory. The traditionalists took the view that toleration implied only a respect for the status quo, the existing social arrangements. Legal status of toleration in Virginia remained uncertain until resolved by the revolutionary Declaration of Rights in 1776.

---

1 Isaac, *Transformation*, p. 63.
2 Gordon S. Wood, *The Radicalism of the American Revolution* (New York: Vintage Books, 1993), p. 18.
3 Isaac, *Transformation*, p. 65
4 Hening, *The Statutes at Large*, 1, pp. 532-533
5 Hening, *The Statutes at Large*, III (1812), p 171. Hening adds this footnote: "It is surely an abuse of terms to call a law a toleration act, which imposes a religious test, on the conscience, in order to avoid the penalties of another law, equally violating every principle of religious freedom."

In the 1740s, as some common people began departing from the established church into congregations of their own making, religion gradually became a major cause of social unrest. Samuel Morris of Hanover County, a brick-layer and a leader of dissent, identified with the New Side Presbyterians in 1743. The "New Side" was an evangelical faction, emphasizing "rebirth." They believed that evidence of conversion for ministers was more important than formal education. This disregard of traditional social authority was more unsettling than the religious doctrine of the dissenters. In 1747, a proclamation from the governor and council called for "all itinerant preachers" to be restrained. Some were called to Williamsburg for trial and fined for unlawful assembly.[1]

In the 1760s, the Baptists became a significant group among dissenters, They faced intense harassment, and by 1771, at least 20 itinerant preachers were put in jail. They refused to give bonds, and sometimes preached through the bars. Between 1769 and 1774 the number of Baptist churches in Virginia increased from seven to 54![2] As the historian Rhys Isaac stated, "Converts were proffered some escape from the harsh realities of disease, debt, overindulgence and deprivation, violence and fear of sudden death, that were the common lot of small farmers."[3] But the traditionalists had only contempt for the ignorant, uneducated Baptist preachers.

During the years just prior to the Revolutionary War, the Baptist rate of increase slowed while the Methodist religion was spreading rapidly. Although the Methodists were similar to the Baptists with their emphasis on close fellowship, emotional sharing and extemporary preaching, they continued to be dependent on clergy ordained by an English bishop. Thus they were not perceived to be as great a threat to the authorities.[4] Nevertheless, these religions that emphasized the individual responsibility of common people continued to undermine deferential faith and obedience.[5]

Then, with the onset of the Revolutionary War, things changed rapidly. In 1776, the future president James Madison amended the English Act of Toleration statement to read "all men should enjoy the free exercise of religion." Just a few months later, a bill was passed that exempted dissenters from being taxed to support the Established Church. There was much controversy and debate over an "Act for Establishing Religious Freedom" that Thomas Jefferson introduced in 1779. It was passed in 1786. As the ties to England were severed by the Revolutionary War, the former Established Church became incorporated as the Protestant Episcopal church.[6]

1　Isaac, *Transformation*, pp. 147-150, 152-153.
2　Wood, *Radicalism*, p. 144.
3　Isaac, *Transformation*, p. 164.
4　Isaac, *Transformation*, pp. 260-261.
5　Wood, *Radicalism*, p. 144.
6　Isaac, *Transformation*, pp. 279-282.

The Cohoke Swamp is located east of Richmond in a curve of the Pamunkey River.

John May, John Baylor, Daniel Coleman, John Madison, Robert Farish, and John Pigg were neighbors living in St. Stephen's Parish in Queen Anne's County.[15] They worshipped together in the parish church, and shared news and views after the Sunday service. They also worked out numerous land deals with each other.

On 20 Oct 1704, John May was granted a headright for land "on branches of the Mattapony." A John Fraser was on the list of persons transported.[16] John Baylor received acreage in "King and Queen County, in St. Stephen's Parish on the north side of the Mattapony river" on 16 Aug 1715. On his list of twenty-seven transported persons

> 13 Aug 1701. "WHEREAS sundry and divers inconveniencies attend the inhabitants of that part of King and Queen county which lies within Pamunkey neck when they have occasion to prosecute law suits . . . or to go to any other publick meeting by reason of the difficulty in passing Matapiny river . . . it is hereby enacted, That from and after the 11th day of April which shall be in the year of our Lord God 1702 the said county of King & Queen be divided into two distinct countyes so that Matapiny river divide the same."
>
> William Walter Hening, *The Statutes at Large: being a Collection of all the Laws of Virginia*, 13 volumes (1823, reprint, Charlottesville, Va.: University Press of Virginia, 1969), 3, p. 211.

---

15 James W. Doyle, Jr., "Saint Stephen's Parish, King and Queen County, James Madison and the Bill of Rights," *Tidewater Virginia Families*, Vol. 5, No.1, pp. 9-17. Doyle has plotted all of the patents in the area.

16 Nugent, *Cavaliers and Pioneers,* III, p. 87. Patent Book 9-619.

were the names of Dunkliant Frazer and Edward Herring.[17]

John Sistlett, Stephen Sistlett, and John Davis were among a group of forty persons transported for a headright claimed in 1714. A patent for 2000 acres in King William County was granted to John Madison and Daniel Coleman. The tract lay "in forke of the Mattapony River, about 4 miles north of Doeg Town,[18] beginning by the North Side of said forke & just below the run of a good spring issuing out of the hills . . . by land of Farrish, Pigg & May."[19]

Ten years later, on 23 Dec 1724, Robert Farish, John Pigg and John May brought Edmund Herring and 39 others to "a fork of Mattapony River, about 2 miles above Doeg Town, beginning in the fork where the two runs meet."[20]

The planters pushed upwards along the rivers to find new land for their tobaco crops. In 1717, John Madison and others patented 1860 acres "in a fork of the Mattapony, about 16 miles above the inhabitants in King and Queen County; beginning about two miles above the stones or falls of the river."[21]

Spotsylvania County was formed in 1721 from the western frontiers of King and Queen, Essex, and King William counties. In 1728, John Madison of King and Queen County bought 1000 acres of new land in Spottsylvania County "at the foot of the Great Mountains."[22]

Could it have been the descendants of these men who lived and

> John Baylor, c.1660–1720, was born in Tiverton, Devonshire, England, but moved to Virginia before 1692. Although he first lived in Gloucester County, by 1714 he had moved to a site on the Mattaponi River in King and Queen County, near the present town of Walkerton. Baylor was one of the greatest merchants, slave traders, and land speculators in the 1710s. He had proposed an expedition to explore and survey the Blue Ridge in 1705 and obtained endorsement and official sanction from the Virginia Council. The expedition didn't materialize. However, after Lt. Governor Alexander Spotswood led his "Knights of the Golden Horseshoe" to the Blue Ridge, his party stayed at Baylor's house on the night of Saturday, 15 Sep 1716, on his return trip to Williamsburg.
>
> John T. Kneebone et al, *Dictionary of Virginia Biography* (Richmond, Va.: The Library of Virginia, 1998), 1, p. 405. Also, Edward P. Alexander, editor, *Journal of John Fontaine* (Williamsburg: Colonial Williamsburg Foundation), p. 108.

---

17 Nugent, *Cavaliers and Pioneers*, III, p. 173. Patent Book 10-250.
18 A settlement of the Doeg Indian tribe, Doeg Town was located near the town of Milford, a few miles southwest of Bowling Green in present Caroline County.
19 Nugent, *Cavaliers and Pioneers*, III, p. 151. This particular abstract does not include the date nor the page number where it is recorded in the deed book. However, several deeds listed before and several after were dated 16 Jun 1714.
20 Nugent, *Cavaliers and Pioneers*, III, p. 167. Deed Book 10, p. 225.
21 Nugent, *Cavaliers and Pioneers*, III, p. 190. Patent Book 10-319.
22 Nugent, *Cavaliers and Pioneers*, III, p. 352. Patent Book 13-351.

The Mattaponi River at the Courthouse Landing in King and Queen County. The rural county still has no incorporated towns, and not a single traffic light!

worked in close proximity in the early 18th century who intermarried and shaped a culture one hundred and two hundred years later? Did the sons and grandsons of indentured servants in the coastal plantations become proud mountain men? Perhaps while the masters gossiped after compulsory church attendance on Sunday, the servants shared their own dreams and made plans. At the end of their indentured terms, did they travel with friends and follow the rivers to their sources in the highlands? Did they continue as paid laborers and overseers on the tobacco plantations? As the large land owners expanded westward, were these experienced workers assigned to till the new land? How and when were they able to acquire land of their own? Unfortunately, the lack of surviving records makes it impossible to document the lives of these men and their families. Few Virginians can trace their ancestry back to an indentured servant. Only a few surviving eighteenth century tax records and court records can help pinpoint an individual at a particular place and time.

> John Madison was a ship's carpenter who immigrated to Virginia in 1653. He settled on the Mattaponi at Mantapike and he acquired 1,900 acres on the York and Mattapony through headrights. His son John was sheriff and justice of the peace in King and Queen County. In 1714, he and a neighbor, Daniel Coleman, patented two thousand acres of land on the upper Mattaponi River, 40 miles above Mantapike. John (II)'s son Ambrose married Francis Taylor, daughter of James Taylor (II). They lived in Montpelier in Orange County, and their son James Madison became the fourth president of the United States.
>
> James Madison University web site.

The early General Assembly of Virginia mandated a Vestry in every parish that had the authority to buy lands for churches, erect buildings, care for the poor and for orphaned children. The vestry was funded from tithes of so many pounds of tobacco per "tithable."[23] This tax usually applied to males sixteen years of age and over, and to servants of both sexes of that age or older.

A John Shiflett was listed as an Orange County tithable in 1737.[24] In 1742, John Shiflett was living in Louisa County "on the south side the Piney Mountain" on land owned by William Coursey. One half of Coursey's 400 acres was sold to Abraham Allen.[25] When Coursey sold the remaining part of the tract to John Dickenson in 1749, the deed specified the portion "where John Shiflet formerly Lived."[26] John had either moved on or died.

A William Frazer was brought into court on 20 Apr 1738 because he had "dangerously wounded one Samuel Rose."[27] He was adjudged to be £40 "in debt to our Sovereign Lord the King."[28] Nine years later a William Frazier was in court again. He was ordered to pay 260 pounds of tobacco to a witness coming seventy miles from Augusta County.[29]

On the 1756 list of Orange County tithables, a John Frazier was described as an overseer. In a will written in 1771, an Alexander Frazier bequeathed "to my friend John Frazier £32 cash if John Frazier should ever appear in person to them that has the money in possession."[30]

---

23 George MacLaren Brydon, *Religious Life of Virginia in the Seventeenth Century* (Williamsburg, Va.: The Virginia 350th Anniversary Celebration Corporation, 1957), p. 13.
24 Barbara Vines Little, compiler, *Orange County Virginia Tithables*, 1734–1782 (Compiler, 1988), Part One, pp. 9-10.
25 Louisa County, Va., Deed Book A-42, recorded 14 Mar 1742.
26 Louisa County, Va., Deed Book A-395, recorded 30 Jan 1749.
27 Orange County, Va., Order Book 1-295.
28 Orange County, Va., Order Book 1-315, court of 25 May 1738.
29 Orange County, Va., Order Book 5-41, court of 17 Aug 1747.
30 Orange County, Va., Will Book 2-431, pr. 23 May 1771.

From the Mattiponi to the Mountains

The quest for land led the 18th century Virginians from the placid waters of the Mattaponi River to the rugged ranges of the Blue Ridge Mountains.

1700s

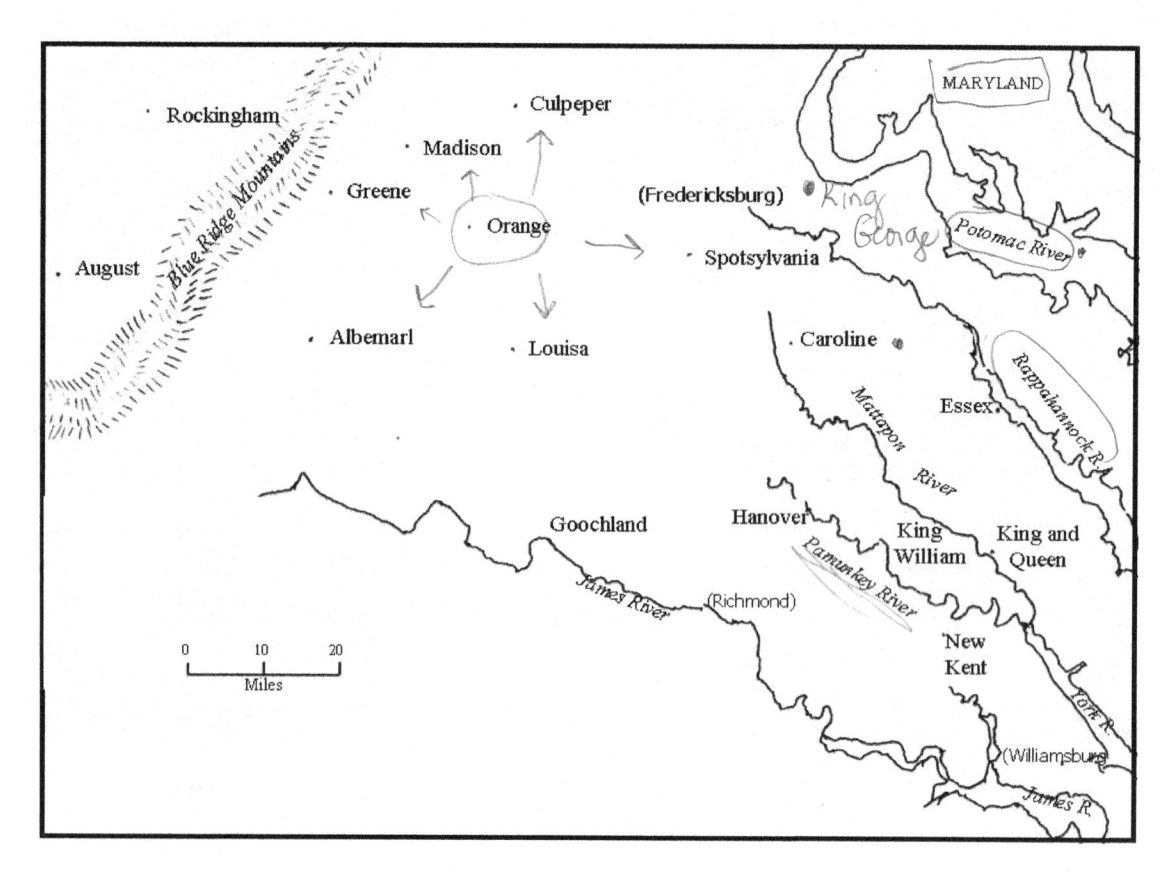

The map above shows the location of relevant county seats from the Mattaponi to the mountains. They are labeled with the county names, which are sometimes, but not always, the same as the town where the courthouse is located. The names of three cities, Richmond, Williamsburg, and Fredericksburg, are placed in parentheses and added as points of reference.

10 Oct 1743

"On petition it is ordered that a road be laid off and cleared from the road in Orange that extends to the dividing line between this County Orange on the river to the upper north fork of Buck mountain creek."

Kathleen R. Perkins, "Abstracts of Law Order Books 1742–1748," *The Louisa County Historical Magazine*, Vol. 10, No. 2, p. 41.

The name of William Morris was on the 1756 list of tithables.[31] In October of 1760, Wm. Herren of Louisa County purchased "One certain tract or parcel of Land containing by Supposition 125 acres . . . Lying and being in Orange County on the foot of the great Mountain on Swift Run."[32] In 1768, the list of tithables in Jeremiah Bryan's precinct included Steaven Shifflet, Wm. Morris, Honorarius Powell, William Shifflet, and several men with the name of Davis.[33]

Stephen Shiflett, of St Thomas Parish, Orange County, bought 100 acres of land from James Powell for £25 on 5 Apr 1771. The tract was described as beginning "at the mouth of a small Branch corner at a poplar two white Oaks & Spanish Oak & turning up the Branch to the head and Cornering at a Poplar again Runing from thence over a small Ridge and Cornering at another poplar at the head of another Small Branch and Runing down the Branch to the great Run and Down the great Run to the Beginning."[34]

These isolated examples show that, despite difficulties with transportation and communication, people were on the move.

Families who shared much of the Shifflett and Morris history for the next 200 years were becoming firmly established in the mountains. Their homes were situated near the lines that divide present Greene County from Albemarle County to the south and Rockingham County at the top of the Blue Ridge.

---

31 Barbara Vines Little, compiler. *Orange County Virginia Tithables*, 1734–1782 (Compiler, 1988), Part One, pp. 41-42.
32 Orange County, Va. Deed Book 13-136, recorded 23 Oct 1760.
33 Little, *Orange County Virginia Tithables*, 1734–1782, p. 98.
34 Orange County, Va. Deed Book 15-332, recorded 25 Apr 1771.

Virginia's 100 counties were formed and subdivided as the population increased and moved into new geographical areas. The county courts were the seat of government and the center of social activity. It was desirable that residents could travel to the county courthouse within a day. In the earliest years, only northern and southern boundaries separated the tidewater counties. What lay to the west was unknown. As new counties were formed in the 18th century, each tended to include "all points west."

Charles River and Henrico were two of eight original shires in 1634. Charles River became **York** in 1643. **New Kent** was formed in 1654 from York County. **King and Queen** was formed from New Kent in 1691. **Hanover** was formed from New Kent in 1720. **Goochland** was formed from Henrico in 1727. **Louisa** was formed from Hanover in 1742. **Albemarle** was formed from Goochland and part of Louisa in 1744.

King William was formed from King and Queen in 1702. **Caroline** was formed from **Essex**, King and Queen and King William in 1727. More of King William County was added later. **Spotsylvania** was formed from Essex, King William, and King and Queen in 1720. **Orange** was formed from Spotsylvania in 1734.

Augusta was formed from Orange in 1738. Because the region was sparsely inhabited, county government was not actually established until 1745. **Culpeper** was formed from Orange in 1749, and **Madison** formed from Culpeper in 1792. **Rockingham** was formed from Augusta in 1778. And, in 1838, the southwestern portion of remaining Orange county was separated to create **Greene** County.

Cutting through the confusion is difficult, but it is easy to see that an eighteenth century family could have lived in several different counties in their lifetime without having moved an inch.

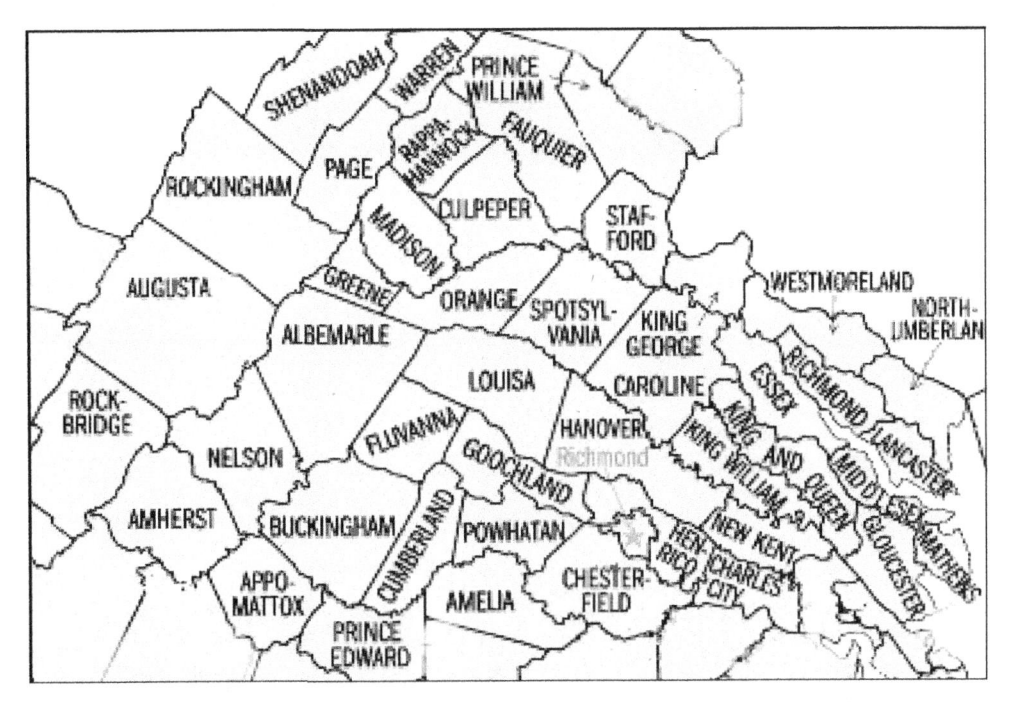

Current boundaries of some central Virginia counties.

   Interpreting the surviving records is a challenge. For example, a person documented in Orange County in 1735 could have been living any place in present Orange, Culpeper, Madison and Greene counties, or over the mountains in Augusta, Rockingham, and all of West Virginia to the Ohio River!

> Emily J. Salmon and Edward D.C. Campbell, editors, *The Hornbook of Virginia History*, fourth edition, (Richmonds, Va.: Library of Virginia. 1994), pp.159-177. Also, Eric G. Grundset, *Historical Boundary Atlas of the Potomac, Shenandoah, and Rappahannock Valleys of Virginia and West Virginia* (Fairfax, Va.: Author, 1999).

3 Cousins on the County Line

The Virginia state census record of 1785[1] lists a John Shifflett living in Albemarle County, in a household with "four white souls," one dwelling and three other buildings.[2] Across the line in Orange County, among families in the precinct enumerated by Jeremiah White,[3] were William Shifflett, with 13 white souls, John Shifflet with 5, Bland Shifflet with 4, William Morris with 8, Thomas Morris with 4, Richard Morris with 7, and another William Morris with 7 white souls.[4] Elizabeth, the widow of Steven Shifflett, was living near her Powell relatives.[5]

These Shiflet men are presumed to be the sons of the John Shiflet in Albemarle County who wrote a will dated 5 Oct 1791.[6] In the will, John bequeaths his "Cattle Hogs Horses Sheep Household Goods" to his unmarried daughter Sarah. He gives his "loving son Blann Shiftlet the Land whereon I now live" with the understanding that Sarah could continue to live there as long as she wished. His other children, John, Stephen, Thomas, William and Richard Shiftlet, Ann Morris and

> Two-thirds of the earliest immigrants to Virginia had lived in the south and west of England. Many were related before they came, and in Virginia they became one of the most intermarried groups ever. The gentility viewed the marriage of cousins as a desirable means of keeping a pure bloodline in the family. In isolated frontier settlements there were other practical considerations. Families were large, but neighbors were few. With each generation there was a diminishing supply of potential spouses who were not related to some degree.
>
> David Hackett Fischer, *Albion's Seed: Four British Folkways in America* (New York: Oxford University Press, 1989), p. 214.

---

1. The 1790 Federal census of Virginia was destroyed by fire.
2. *Heads of Families, Virginia: Records of the State Enumerations, 1782–1785* (Washington, D.C.: 1908), p. 80.
3. The area would become Greene County in 1838.
4. *State Enumerations, 1782–1785*, p. 96. The Morris families are discussed in Chapter 4.
5. *State Enumerations, 1782–1785*, p. 97.
6. Frederick Parish, Albemarle County, Va., Will of John Shiftlet, dated 5 Oct 1791, pr. 1 Dec 1806. Virginia State Library, Unrecorded Deeds of Albemarle County, 1785–1812, microfilm reel 216. This will was discovered, transcribed, and shared by Larry Shifflett. It was submitted to the Shiflett Family Genealogy website. Many researchers have contributed information on early Shiflets to this excellent website.

Susannah Morris, "have already received their parts." His sons William and Richard Shiftlet were named executors. The will was proved in court on 1 Dec 1806.

The children listed below should be designated as probable. There is no doubt that John had a child of that name, but there is insufficient proof in all cases that the person described is the "right one" bearing that name.

Children of John Shiflet and ___ ___

1. John   – pr. Oct 1794   m. Joice Powell

   b

   d Albemarle County, Va., Will Book 3-230. Will of John Shiflett, dated 7 Sep 1794, mentions his wife Joice. His daughter Mary was to receive the tract where he lived and a Negro woman named Jane. After his wife's death, John specified that his estate should be divided among "all my children." Pr. Oct 1794. Numerous Albemarle County land transactions attest to the prosperity of this John Shiflet.

   m Culpepper County, Va., Will Book B-140. An administrative account of the estate of John Powell, deceased, was brought to the court on 25 Aug 1766. A distribution of £19.2.10 was made to John Shiflet.

2. Stephen   – pr. 17 Dec 1776   m. Elizabeth Powell

   b Stephen was listed as a tithable in Orange County in 1768. Barbara Vines Little, compiler. *Orange County Virginia Tithables, 1734–1782* (Compiler, 1988), p. 98.

   d Orange County, Va., Will Book 3-136. An administration account of the estate of Stephen Shiflet, deceased, was presented to the court on 17 Dec 1766.

   m Culpepper County, Va., Will Book B-140. An administrative account of the estate of John Powell, deceased, was brought to the court on 25 Aug 1766. A distribution of £19.2.10 was made to Stephen Shiflet.

3. Thomas [52][7]   c.1733 – after 1799   m. Patience ____

   b Thomas was 21 years old at the time of his service in the French and Indian War. "Virginia Military Records," from *The Virginia Magazine of History and Biography*, the *William and Mary College Quarterly*, and *Tyler's Quarterly*. (Baltimore: Genealogical Publishing, 1983), p. 364.

   d Mentioned in the will of his father, John Shiftlet, dated 5 Oct 1791. No record of Thomas' death has been found.

   m The names of Thomas and Patience appear together on a 1799 list of members of the Buck Mountain Baptist Church. Library of Virginia, Albemarle County miscellaneous microfilm, reel 472, page 60 0f section.

---

7 The numbers in brackets identify ancestors on the family trees in Appendix A, pages 137 and 139. Note that each father's number is twice that of his child; the mother's number is twice plus one.

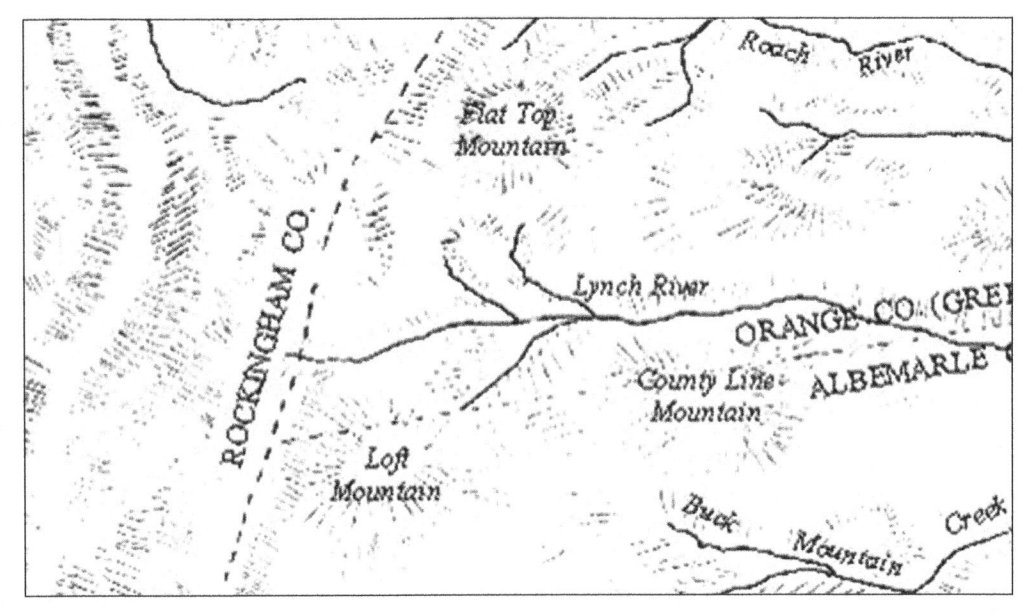

The farms of John Shiflet and his sons, frequently referred to as "plantations" in the early years, were located in the northwestern corner of Albemarle County and across the line in Orange County.

4. Richard [16*][8] – pr. 2 Mar 1830

- b 1820 U.S. census, Albemarle County, Va., page numbers torn (surnames arranged alphabetically by first letter), micropublication M33, roll 130. A Richard Shiflet, Sr., "over 45," was listed. This may have been the son of Thomas [52].

- d Albemarle County, Va., Will Book 10-42, dated 27 Jan 1827, pr. 2 Mar 1830.

- m Richard's will mentions children: Nathaniel, William, Blan, and John. His son William is believed to be the William Shiflett [8*] who died in 1845 (Greene County, Va., Will Book 1-144, dated 20 Jun 1843). One of his sons was William "Buck" Shifflett [4*], c.1808–1881. See Chapter 6.

5. William [86]

- b A William Shifflit was a tithable in Orange County in 1766 and 1768. (Little, Orange County Virginia Tithables, pp. 84, 98.)

- d

- m Molly Shiflet [43], a daughter of William Shiflet, married William Herring [42] on 1 Feb 1788. (Albemarle County, Va., Marriage Register, 1, 1780–1805, p. 140.) Their daughter Joice Herring [21] was the wife of Edward Shiflett [20]. See Chapter 6.

---

8 An asterisk after the identification number indicates a probable but not proven ancestor.

> "The soil below the mountains seems to have acquired a character for goodness which it by no means deserves. Though not rich, it is well suited to the growth of tobacco and Indian corn, and some parts of it for wheat. Good crops of cotton, flax, and hemp, are also raised; and in some counties they have plenty of cider, and exquisite brandy, distilled from peaches, which grow in great abundance on the numerous rivers of the Chesapeak."
> Morse, Geography Made Easy, 1802, p. 219.

6. Bland [54]   c.1751 – 15 Jul 1840   m. Vina _____

   b

   d   The date of his death and his age at the time were written opposite his name on the census of 1840. (1840 U.S. census, Greene County, Va., p. 434 (stamped), National Archives micropublication 704, roll 559.)

   m   "An indenture of bargain and sale between Bland Shifflett and Vina, his wife of the one part and William McGhee of the other part was produced unto Court and acknowledged by Bland Shiflett party hereto and the relinquishment of Dower of the said Vina in the lands conveyed by the Indenture taken in open Court and ordered to be recorded." Dated 1 Dec 1806, Albemarle County, Va., Order Book 1806–1807, p. 23.

7. Ann   m. Richard Morris

   b   Mentioned in the will of her father, John Shiftlet, dated 5 Oct 1791.

   d   An inventory of the estate of Richard Morris was taken on 30 Mar 1815. Orange County, Va., Will Book 5-47.

   m   Orange County deeds from the 1790s (e.g., Deed Books 20-145; 21-188; 21-192) indicate that Richard and Ann had land along Roach River and on Naked Mountain.

8. Susannah   m. _____ Morris

   b

   d

   m   Frederick Parish of Albemarle County, Va., will of John Shiftlet, dated 5 Oct 1791, indicates that Susannah was married to a Morris.

9. Sarah   unmarried

   b

   d

   m   Frederick Parish of Albemarle County, Va., will of John Shiftlet, dated 5 Oct 1791, pr. 1 Dec 1806.

Children of Bland Shiflett [54] and Vina ___ [55]

1. Bland, Jr.   – d. before 1860   m. Elizabeth Shiflett

   b

   d   L. F. Shifflett and Barbara Shifflett Hensley, compilers and editors, *Shifflet vs. Shifflett: A Greene County, Virginia, Chancery Cause, 1860–1879* (compilers, 1996), p. 65. The authors analyze family relationships in a discussion of the heirs and devisees of Stephen Palmer Shiflett.

   m   John Vogt and T. William Kethley, Jr., *Albemarle County Marriages, 1780–1853*, 3 volumes (Athens, Ga.: Iberian Publishing Company, 1991), p. 283. On 9 Sep 1791, Bland Shiflett m. Elizabeth Shiflett, d/o William Shiflett. Wit: William Herring, James Hearing.

2. John S. B.   – d. early 1859   m. Rhoda Shiflett

   b

   d   Shifflett and Hensley, *Shifflet vs. Shifflett: A Greene County, Virginia, Chancery Cause*, p. 65.

   m   Vogt, John, and T. William Kethley, Jr. *Orange County Marriages, 1747–1850*. Revised edition. Athens, Ga.: Iberian Publishing Company, 1990, p. 109. On 29 Dec 1798, John S. B. Shiflet and Rhoda Shiflet were married by the minister George Bingham.

3. Stephen Palmer Shiflet   c.1780 –   unmarried

   b   1850 U.S. census, Greene County, Va., page 341 (stamped), dwelling 36, family 36; micropublication M432, reel 947. Stephen Shiflett, 70.

   d

   m   Shifflett and Hensley, *Shifflet vs. Shifflett: A Greene County, Virginia, Chancery Cause*, p. 60.

4. Anna [27]   c.1781 – before 1853   m. Larkin Shiflett

   b   1850 U.S. census, Greene County, Virginia, page 347 (stamped), dwelling 113, family 113; National Archives micropublication M432, roll 947. Enumeration date 17 Aug 1850. Larkin Shiflett, 69, Anna, 69.

   d   Greene County, Va., Register of Deaths, p. 2. When Larkin Shiflett died in 1853, he was unmarried, thus suggesting that Anna predeceased him.

   m   Shifflett and Hensley, *flet vs. Shifflett: A Greene County, Virginia, Chancery Cause*, p. 63.

5. Overton   c.1783 – pr. 15 Jun 1864   m. Sarah E. Herring

   b   1860 U.S. census, Greene County, Va., page 36, dwelling 282, family 282; micropublication M653, roll 1349. Overton Shiflet, 77.

   d   Greene County, Va. Will Book 2-60, dated 26 Aug 1859, pr. 15 Jun 1864. His will mentioned his wife Sally and children Lucinda Herring, Polly Shiflett, Cally Shiflett, Early Shiflett, Emily, Henderson, and Giney. All of the children were bequeathed significant amounts of land. Also, see Shifflett and Hensley, *Shifflet vs. Shifflett: A Greene County, Virginia, Chancery Cause*, p. 62. Overton was deceased shortly before 16 Nov 1863.

   m   Vogt and Kethley, *Orange County Marriages, p. 109*. Overton Shifflet m. Sally Herring, d/o William R. Herring on 19 Jan 1809.

6. Nancy   c.1784 –   m. John Morris

   b   1860 U.S. census, Greene County, Va., page 36, dwelling 286, family 286; micropublication M653, roll 1349. John Morris, Sr., 77, Nancy, 76.

   d

   m   Vogt and Kethley, Albemarle County Marriages, 1, p. 233. The Methodist minister, John Gibson, married Nancy Shifflet and John Morriss on 3 May 1804.

7. Absalom   c.1790 –   m.? Winny Herring

   b   1850 U.S. census, Albemarle County, Va., page 185 (stamped), dwelling 414, family 414; National Archives micropublication M432, roll 932. Absalom Shifflett, 60.

   d

   m   There is no evidence that Absalom and Winny were married. Their children sometimes used the name Shiflett, sometimes Herring, e.g., the Nicholas Shifflet/Herring who married Nancy Lawson (see Chapter 5). Winny was a sister of Joice Herring [21] (see Chapter 6).

8. Mildred (Milly)   c.1793 –   m. Winston Shifflet

   b   1850 U.S. census, Greene County, Va., page 342 (stamped), dwelling 69, family 69; micropublication M432, roll 947. Winston Shifflett, 58, Milly, 57.

   d

   m   Shifflett and Hensley, *Shifflet vs. Shifflett: A Greene County, Virginia, Chancery Cause*, p. 62.

9. James   c.1795 – 12 Oct 1869   m. Mildred Herrin

   b   1860 U.S. census, Greene County, Va., dwelling 180, family 180; micropublication M653, roll 1349. Jas Shiflet, 65.

   d   Greene County, Va., Death Register.

   m   Vogt and Kethley, *Orange County Marriages*, p. 108. James Shifflet and Milly Herrin were married on 5 Jul 1815.

10. Vina   c.1800 –   m. John Shiflett

   b   1850 U.S. census, Greene County, Va., page 344 (stamped), dwelling 75, family 75; micropublication 432, roll 947. John Shiflett, 55, Vina, 50. 1860 U.S. census, Greene County, Va., p. 42, dwelling 167, family 167; micropublication 653, roll 1349. John Shifflet, Sr. 65, Vina, 60.

   d

   m   Vogt and Kethley, *Orange County Marriages*, p. 231. On 24 Dec 1816, Vina Shifflet and John Shifflet were married by the minister George Bingham.

11. Pleasant   c. 1800 – before 1850   m. Mary Powell

   b

   d 1850 U.S. census, Rockingham County, Va., 56 1/2 district, page 184 (stamped), dwelling 172, family 177; micropublication 432, roll 974. Mary Shiflet, 50, was head of the household.

   m Vogt and Kethley, *Orange County Marriages,* p. 109. Pleasant Shiflett and Mary Powell were married by George Bingham on 11 Jan 1827.

The story of Anna Shiflett [27] who married her cousin Larkin Shiflett [26] is continued on page 35.

Thomas Shiflett [52]

> Only land owners fought in colonial Virginia's wars. Slaves and indentured servants were not even included in the county enlistments.
>
> Rhys Isaac, *The Transformation of Virginia, 1740–1790* (New York: W. W. Norton, 1982), p. 105.

Thomas Shiflett [52] was an older brother of Bland Shiflett [54]. The earliest documentation of Thomas is a record of his service in the French and Indian War. An undated "Size Roll of Major Andrew Lewis' Company" reveals personal information: Thos. Shifflet, age 21, 5 feet, 10½ inches, Trade: Planter, Country: Virginia, Where Entertained: Louisa County.[9] Thomas lived in the portion of Louisa County which later became Albemarle County. The location of his farm is indicated on a 1773 survey: "A plat of 187 acres of land 182 acres of which lies in Albemarle County the other 5a in Orange. On the County line mountain in the waters of Buck mountain creek & Lynch's river. Survey'd for Thomas Shiflet 29th March 1773."[10]

Thomas Shiflett and his wife Patience attended the Buck Mountain Baptist Church. They were listed on—and crossed off of—"A fresh Collection of the names of the white persons in the Baptist Church now in fellowship and under care. Taken this 21st Day of April 1799."[11]

---

  9 "Virginia Military Records," from *The Virginia Magazine of History and Biography, the William and Mary College Quarterly, and Tyler's Quarterly.* (Baltimore: Genealogical Publishing, 1983), p. 364.

10 Albemarle County, Va., Surveyor's Book, No. 1, Part 2, p. 99. For additional information on Thomas Shiflett's land, see the Shiflet Genealogy Website.

11 Library of Virginia, Albemarle County miscellaneous microfilm, reel 472, p. 60

Children of Thomas Shiflett [52] and Patience ___ [53]

1. Richard   c. 1765 – 22 Jan 1855   m. Elizabeth Snow

    b 1850 U.S. census, Greene County, Va., p. 341 (stamped), dwelling 37, family 37; micropublication M432, reel 947. Richard Shiflett, 85, Elizabeth, 83.

    d County, Va., Death Register, p. 6. 22 Jan 1855, Richard Shiflett, age 93, husband of Elizabeth, son of Thomas and Patience, born in Albemarle County. Information given by a friend John Gentry.

    m County, Va., Death Register, p. 3. 23 May 1854, Elizabeth Shiflett, age 98, w/o Richard, d/o Thomas and Molly Snow. Information given by her son Benson Shiflett.

2. Larkin [26]   c.1778 – bef. 26 Feb 1853   m. Anna Shiflett

    b 1850 U.S. census, Greene County, Virginia, page 347 (stamped), dwelling 113, family 113; National Archives micropublication M432, roll 947. Larkin Shiflett, 69, Anna, 69.

    d "List of Property belonging to the Estate of Larkin Shiflett Dec'd." was written on 26 Feb 1853 and submitted to the Court on 17 Mar 1853. (Greene County, Va., Will Book 1-438.) A later death date is recorded in the Greene County, Va., Register of Deaths, p. 2. Larkin Shiflett, age 75, s/o Thomas and Patience Shiflett, died 6 Jul 1853 of dropsy.

    m L. F. Shifflett and Barbara Shifflett Hensley, compilers and editors, *Shiflett vs. Shiflett: A Greene County, Virginia, Chancery Cause, 1860–1879* (Compilers, 1996), p. 63. Anna was a daughter of Bland and Vina Shiflett, thus a first cousin of Larkin.

3. Thomas   – d. 14 Mar 1823   m. Elizabeth (Betty) Lamb

    b

    d L. F. Shifflett and Barbara Shifflett Hensley, compilers and editors, *Shiflet (and variant spellings) 1700–1900* (Compilers, 1995), p. 73. Thomas Shifflet, Jr. died in Madison County, Kentucky.

    m John Vogt and T. William Kethley, Jr., *Albemarle County Marriages, 1780–1853*, 3 volumes, Athens, Ga.: Iberian Publishing Company, 1991), p. 285. The marriage bond of Thomas Shiflett and Betty Lamb was signed on 15 May 1790. She was the d/o Richard Lamb.

4. John   – pr. 22 Nov 1830   m. Susanna Davis

    b

    d Orange County, Va., Will Book 7-275, will of John Shiflett written in 1829, pr. 22 Nov 1830.

    m John Vogt and T. William Kethley, Jr., *Orange County Marriages, 1747–1850*, revised edition (Athens, Ga.: Iberian Publishing Company, 1990), p. 109. John Shiflett and Susanna Davis were married on 27 Oct 1796 by the minister George Bingham. Susanna was a daughter of Lewis Davis. Orange County, Va., Will Book 6-357, dated 4 May 1819.

Larkin Shiflett [26]

Larkin Shiflett [26], son of Thomas and Patience Shiflett, was born in Albemarle County about 1778. He married his cousin Anna Shiflett [27]. Larkin Shiffalette was granted a 50-acre tract of land "in the big mountains" in Orange County on 13 Jun 1820. It was situated on the south side of Fork Mountain.[12]

> Thomas M Randolph Esq. Governor of the Commonwealth of Virginia To all whom these presents shall come Greeting
>
> Know ye that in conformity with a survey made on the Thirteenth of May 1819; by virtue of a Land Office Treasury Warrant Number 6524 issued the 6th February 1819, there is granted by the said Commonwealth unto Larkin Shiffalette A certain tract or parcel of Land containing fifty acres situate in the county of Orange in the Big mountain and bounded as followeth to wit.
>
> Beginning at two Chestnut Oaks on the South side of Fork mountain running thence North seven degrees West sixty eight to a large Chestnut Oak thence North seven degrees East twelve poles to two Chestnut Oaks, thence North eighty three degrees East twelve poles to two Chestnut Oaks thence North seven degrees West ninety two poles to a large white Oak Chestnut and Spanish Oak on the East side of said mountain, thence South eighty three degrees West fifty five poles to a large red Oak Spanish Oak and hickory sapling thence South seven degrees East one hundred and sixty poles to a chestnut amongst some rocks and thence North eighty three degrees East forty four poles to the beginning. To have and to hold the said tract or parcel of land with its appertenances unto the said Larkin Shiffalette and his heirs forever. In witness whereof the said Thomas M. Randolph Esq. Governor of the Commonwealth of Virginia hath hereunto set his Hand and cause the lesser Seal of the said Commonwealth to be affixed at Richmond on the Thirteenth day of June in the year of our Lord One thousand eight hundred and twenty and of the Commonwealth the fortyfourth.
>
> Tho M. Randolph

On 16 Sep 1836, he purchased "the land where Shiflett now lives" from James Sims. This tract of 100 acres was described as "Beginning at the fork of Roaches river thence up the west prong to Michael Cattertons line thence with sd line to Sullivans line to the north prong of sd river to the beginning."[13]

As was true of so many others in the area, Larkin was beset by hard financial times in the 1840s. His land and personal property were put in a deed of trust because "The said Larkin Shiflette is justly indebted to the said Elizabeth Shiflette in the sum of Eighty dollars for four years Services, & to Oversheets Shifflette in the sum of one hundred twenty-five dollars for five years Services, & to Polly Garrett in the sum of twenty

---

12 Virginia Land Office Grants No. 69, 1819–1820, p. 178 (reel 135).
13 Orange County, Va. Deed Book 36-233, recorded 20 Sep 1836.

dollars & to Thornton Mooney in the sum of two dollars & .50 to Parrotte Elliot."[14]

In return for $1 paid to Larkin, the deed directed trustee James Chapman to be custodian of

> One tract of land on which the said Larkin now lives on containing one hundred & fifty acres with its appurtenances thereto belonging. Three loads of furniture sticks $6, one loom, one Coton wheel, one flax wheel, 2 pots and 1 oven, 1/2 doz pewter plats, 1/2 doz earthen plates, 1/2 doz Cups & Saucers, 2 Pottle[?] basins, 2 paint[?] basins, 4 knivs & six forks, 2 dist[?] dishes, 4 killing hogs, 2 ancs[?] & one hatchet, 2 pairs of pot hooks, 2 cows & one calf, 8 head of hogs, 1 bay mare, 2 pairs of pot hooks, 2 plow hors and one stock, one Colter plow, 2 chest, one bureau, 2 old cupboards, one pullay bar & 2 locks, 2 sets of plow gears, 8 chairs, 5 cider barrls. & 2 old hogsheads and 1/2 doz earthen boles and 5 jugs.

But if all of the debts are paid before 1 Aug 1853, "then this indenture to be void."

At the time of the 1850 census, both Larkin and Anna were listed as 69 years of age. Three minor children were in the household: Elizabeth, 17; James A., 9; and Henry, age 5. Two adult children, Overstreet, age 44, and Matilda, age 32, both categorized as "idiotic," were also living with their parents.[15]

A cousin, John Shiflett, reported that Larkin Shiflett was 75 years old when he died of dropsy (congestive heart failure) on 6 Jul 1853.[16] He provided the information that Larkin was a son of Thomas and Patience Shiflett, and was born in Albemarle County. Larkin was unmarried, thus suggesting that his wife preceded him in death.

There appears to have been an error in reporting or recording the date of death. An appraisal of the deceased man's belongings was made five months earlier, on 26 Feb 1853!

List of Property belonging to the Estate of Larkin Shiflett Dec'd.

1 old Shotgun $3. 1 bed stead & a feather tick 1 sheet & [?] [?] coverlit $10	$13.00
1 bureau & [?] $9 1 bed stead 1 feather tick & sheet & coverlet $8	
1 kitchen crock .75	17.75
1 walnut chest $2.50 1 Rim cupboard $1 1 small bay Mair $35	
1 whole corn $17	55.50
1 red cow & bull $13 1 white yearling $3 1 pided[?] yearling $4 3 Hogs $1	21.00
1 pine table .25 cider 23 gallons 2.50 1 empty cider barrel .38	3.08
1 old pine cupboard $1 1 cider barrel at Harry Shiflets .75 1 blue Sow? $4	5.75
1 small barrel .50 1 large auger .50 1 Iron wedge .33	1.33
1 small black Shoat $2 3 guns .37 4 split bottom chairs .50 1 old Couch pot & hooks track .75 1 iron old cook pot .12	2.87

---

14 Greene County, Va. Deed Book 3-397, dated and recorded 13 Aug 1847.
15 1850 U.S. census, Greene County, Virginia, page 347 (stamped), dwelling 113, family 113; National Archives micropublication M432, roll 947.
16 Greene County, Va., Register of Deaths, p. 2

2 Bibles & 1 of Wesley's sermons books 1.25	$2.12
Amount	$122.40

In Greene County Court 17th March 1853.
This appraisement was this day returned to the Court & ordered to be recorded.[17]

Of particular interest are the Bibles and Larkin's book of Wesley's sermons. Could he read them? Although Larkin signed deeds with his mark, indicating limited penmanship ability, he may have had some reading instruction from family or a neighbor.

A deed of trust continued to provide for his son Overstreet after Larkin's death. On 16 Mar 1854,

> James Chapman, Trustee (acting under a deed of trust) made to him in the year 1847 by Larkin Shiflette for the benefit of Overstreet Shiflett . . . to Overton Shiflett curator of Overstreet Shiflett a son of Larkin Shifflett named in said deed of his father Larkin Shiflett to said James Chapman. Witnesseth that in consideration of one dollar in hand paid by the said Overton Shifflett and also in consideration that the one hundred and fifty dollars the amount of Overstreet's interest mentioned in the trust deed of Larkin Shiflett gave for fifty acres of land. The said James Chapman as trustee aforesaid doth grant to the said Overton Shiflett fifty acres of land . . . for the benefit of said Overstreet Shiflett which said land belonged to the estate of Larkin Shiflett dec'd, and includes the mountain lands of said Larkin Shiflett, Sr in the county of Greene, adjoining the lands of John Shiflett & others & and bounded as follows: Beginning at 1. [?] [?] [?]on the N prong of Lynch river in said John Shifletts line, and with his line S. 75 W 8 poles to 2.a poplar & hickory in said line in a prong of said river up the meanders of said river N 61 W poles N 44 W 24 poles N. 24 W 16 poles, N 68 W 25 poles, N 32, W 14 poles N 77 W 16 poles, N 84, W 54 poles to 3. two elms in said prong among some large rocks, thence N 68 E 144 poles to 4. a dogwood, pine and oak on the N prong of Lynch River – Then with said prong S. 9: E 133 poles to the beginning containing fifty acres.[18]

The burial sites of Larkin Shiflett [26] and his wife Anna [27] are unknown.

---

17 Greene County, Va., Will Book 1-438.
18 Greene County, Va. Deed Book 4-409.

Children of Larkin Shiflett [26] and Anna Shiflett [27]

1. Peachy [13] 1799 – August 1884 m. Jeremiah Morris

    b 1860 U.S. census, Greene County, Virginia, Swift Run District, page 24, dwelling 186, family 186; National Archives micropublication 653, roll 1349. J. Morris, 60, Peachy, 61.

    d Greene County Court House, Register of Deaths, p. 21. Peachy Morris died 1 Aug 1884. Cause of death unknown. Age 85. Parents: L. and A. Shiflett. Occupation: labor. Consort of J. Morris. Person giving information: S. Morris, son.

    m Orange County, Va., Marriage Bonds, 10-291, Minister's Return of George Bingham. On 28 Sep 1824, Jeremiah Morris married Peachy Shifflet.

2. Fielding c.1808 – after 1880 m. Elizabeth Shiflett

    b 1850 U.S. census, Albemarle County, Va., page 184 (stamped), dwelling 402, family 202, National Archives micropublication M432, roll 932, Fielding Shifflett, 42, Elizabeth, 33.

    d 1880 U.S. census, Albemarle County, Va., page 438, National Archives micropublication T9, roll 1631. Feling Shifflett, age 65.

    m John Vogt and T. William Kethley, Jr., *Albemarle County Marriages, 1780–1853,* 3 volumes (Athens, Ga.: Iberian Publishing Company, 1991), 1, p. 284. Minister John Gibson married Fielding Shiflett and Betsy Shiflett about 27 Oct 1834.

3. Overstreet c.1806 –

    b 1850 U.S. census, Greene County, Virginia, page 347 (stamped), dwelling 113, family 113; National Archives micropublication M432, roll 947. Overstreet, age 44, idiotic. In 1860, "Street," age 50, was living in the household of Wm. Rodgers (1860 U.S. census, Greene County, Va., page 74, dwelling 593, family 593; micropublication M653, roll 1349).

    d

    m

4. Vina c.1812 – m. Loudon B. Bruce

    b 1850 U.S. census, Greene County, Va., page 342 (stamped), dwelling 57, family 57; micropublication M432, roll 947. Loudon B. Bruce, 68, Lina, 38. Vina and L. B. Bruce are both listed as age 70 in the 1860 Greene County census (Family 197 on micropublication M653, roll 1349). Either this is an error in age or they are not the same persons. Larkin would not have had a child at age 12.

    d

    m Vogt and Kethley, Jr., *Albemarle County Marriages,* 2, p. 626. Sina [Vina] Shiflett and Loudon B. Bruce were married by John Gibson on 30 Apr 1837.

5. Matilda   c.1818 –

- b   1850 U.S. census, Greene County, Virginia, page 347 (stamped), dwelling 113, family 113; National Archives micropublication 432, roll 947. Matilda, age 32, idiotic.
- d
- m   In the 1850 Greene County census, Matilda and three minor children are listed as living in the home of Matilda's parents. No marriage record has been found.

6. Milley   c.1820 –   m. Henderson Shifflett

- b   1850 U.S. census, Greene County, Virginia, page 345 (stamped), dwelling 84, family 84; National Archives micropublication 432, roll 947. Henderson Shiflett, 34; Milley Shiflett, 25. However, in the 1840 census (Greene County, Virginia, page 435 (stamped), National Archives micropublication 704, roll 559), the household of Henderson Shiflett had only one male and one female, both between the ages of 20-30.
- d
- m   Vogt and Kethley, Jr., *Albemarle County Marriages*, 2, p. 625. Milley Shifflett and Henderson Shifflett were married on 22 Dec 1837 by minister John Gibson. Her father, Larkin Shiflett gave his consent.

7. Adam Linneaus   c.1825 –   m. Cally Shiflett

- b   Greene County, Virginia, page 345 (stamped), dwelling 184, family 84; National Archives micropublication 432, roll 947. Lineaa, age 25, and Calla, 30, were living in the household of Henderson Shiflett. 1860 U.S. census, Greene County, Virginia, page 42, dwelling 168, family 168; National Archives micropublication M653, roll 1349. "Laru," 38, Caly, 40.
- d
- m   Eugene D. Powell, *Marriage Records of Greene County, Virginia, 1838–1900* (Quinque, Va.: Compiler, 1998), p. 3. Adam Shiflett, s/o Larkin and Anna Shiflett, age 19, m. Cally Shiflett, d/o Overton and Sarah Shiflett, age 24, on 17 Dec 1844.

The story of Peachy Shiflett [13] who married Jeremiah Morris [12] is continued on page 51.

4 A Farm on Flat Gut Run

The common English surname Morris is derived from the word "Moorish" and is thought to have been originally applied to those with a dark, swarthy complexion.[1]

Many Morris immigrants came into the English colonies. A William Morris acquired vast land holdings in Virginia. On 20 Feb 1723 he received a patent for 1,850 acres in Hanover County "on the lower side of Taylor's Creek, beginning at George Alves'[2] upper corner the same now belonging to sd William Morris & George Dabney."[3]

By the middle of the 18th century, there were Morris families living in many Virginia counties. For example, a Thomas Morris was one of the first five constables appointed in Spotsylvania County in 1722.[4] When he died in 1742 he left a son William.[5] Sylvanus Morris was a Quaker living in Louisa County.[6] Samuel Morris was a bricklayer in Hanover County who, after a religious awakening, led ordinary people in early dissent against the Church of England.[7] In 1743, Morris and his followers identified themselves as Presbyterians.

And there was the servant William Morris belonging to James Woodward who was brought before the Orange County court on 25 May 1738 "for absenting himself from his Masters Service." The court judged that "for absenting himself two and twenty days . . . that he serve him for the Same three months and Sixteen days after the time of his service is expired."[8]

A William Morris was named as a tithable in Orange County on the 1756 list. In 1757, Wm. Morris with a household of eight tithables was delinquent in paying his

---

[1] P. H. Reaney and R. M. Wilson, *A Dictionary of English Surnames*, 3rd revised edition (London: Routledge, 1991), p. 303.
[2] Alves had obtained a patent in 1714 (Patent Book 10-212) for the importation of "Jno. Sislett and Stephen Sislett."
[3] Library of Virginia Digital Images: Land Office Records, Patent Book 11-325.
[4] James Roger Mansfield, *A History of Early Spotsylvania* (Orange, Va.: Green Publishers, 1977), p. 115.
[5] William A. Crozier, editor, *Spotsylvania County Records, 1721–1800: Transcriptions from the Original Files at the County Court House . . .* (Baltimore: Southern Book Co.,1955), p. 6. Abstract of Spotsylvania County, Va.,Will Book A-343, pr. 6 Apr 1742.
[6] Nancy Baird and Kate Hatch, *Abstracts of Louisa County, Virginia Will Books, 1743–1801* (Compilers, 1964), p. 3.
[7] Rhys Isaacs, *The Transformation of Virginia, 1740–1790* (New York: W. W. Norton, 1982), p. 148.
[8] Orange County, Va., Order Book 1-316.

tithes. The next year, a Wm. Morris had only three tithables.[9] In 1767 and 1768, just before the law limiting the number of tobacco plants allowed per person was repealed, the name of Wm. Morris, Senior was written on "Jeremiah Bryan his List of Sucker hunting tiths."[10]

William Morris of Orange County purchased 400 acres along the Roach River from "James Taylor, Gent. of Orange." This tract adjoined Matthew Creed and Honorias Powell. Taylor held a mortgage on the property "in consideration of the sum Quantity of Sixteen Thousand pounds of Crop Tobacco to be paid in Fredericksburgh or Roustons[?] Warehouses each Hogshead to weigh Eleven hundred pounds Nett."[11].

. . . Nevertheless if the said William Morris his heirs etc. shall well and Truly pay or cause to be paid unto the said James Taylor his heirs and Assigns the above sum of Sixteen Thousand pounds of Crop Tobacco as above said with interest on four Thousand pounds of Tobo from the Tenth day of April one Thousand Seven hundred and Seventy one till paid also interest on four thousand pounds of Tobo more from the 10th day of April 1772 till paid Also Interest on four thousand pounds of Tobo more from the Tenth day of April 1773 till paid Also Interest on four thousand pounds of Tobo more from the Tenth day April 1774 till paid. then this indenture shall cease and be Void Anything herein to the contrary notwithstanding. In Witness whereof the said William Morris hath set his hand and Seal the day and year above written.

> By the middle of the 18th century, Scottish merchants had set up warehouses and stores in Fredericksburg, Culpeper, and Caroline Court House. They bought the farmers' tobacco outright (not on consignment), sold them imported goods, and extended credit. This direct dealing reduced dependence on the large Tidewater plantation owners as middlemen.
>
> Jacob M. Price, "The Rise of Glasgow in the Chesapeake Tobacco Trade, 1707–1775," *William and Mary Quarterly*, 3rd series, XI (April 1954), pp. 179-199.

William Morris signed in his own hand. In a separate deed, written the same day, James Taylor attested that he is "fully satisfied and paid," and William Morris is discharged from the mortgage.[12] Just 10 years later, William Morris and his wife Mary sold the same 400 acres back to James Taylor for 16,000 pounds of tobacco![13] However, because William Morris' wife Mary could not "conveniently travel to our County Court of Orange to make Acknowledgement" the deed could not

---

9 Barbara Vines Little, compiler, *Orange County Virginia Tithables, 1734–1782* (Compiler, 1988), pp. 41, 48 and 56.
10 Little, *Orange County Virginia Tithables*, pp. 91 and 98. On p. 211, Little states that the law regarding tobacco suckers was repealed in 1769.
11 Orange County, Va., Deed Book 15-277, dated 5 Mar 1771, recorded 28 Mar 1771.
12 Orange County, Va., Deed Book 15-278, dated 5 Mar 1771, recorded 28 Mar 1771.
13 Orange County, Va., Deed Book 18-49, dated 20 Apr 1782, recorded 23 May 1783.

A view of Bacon Hollow from the Skyline Drive overlook. The Roach River can be seen meandering into the distance. Flat Gut Run is in the hollow beyond the first ridge on the right.

be recorded until representatives of the court questioned her.

> By virtue of the Commission hereunto annexed we the subscribers did on the 19th day of May 1783 go to the within Mary Morriss and having examined her Privately and apart from William Morriss her husband do certifie that she Declared that it was without the Persuasion of threats of her husband she voluntarily and freely acknowledge the Conveyance contained in the Indenture here annexed and that she was willing the same should be recorded in the County Court of Orange. Witness our hands and seals the 19th day of May 1783.[14]

The relationship, if any, of this William and Mary to future Morris generations along "Roaches" River is unknown. The state census of 1785 listed two William Morris households in Orange County, one having eight "white souls," the other seven.[15] One of those men was the probable progenitor of all the Morris families in Bacon Hollow.[16]

---

14 Orange County, Va., Deed Book 18-52, dated 19 May 1783, recorded 23 May 1783.
15 *Heads of Families, Virginia: Records of the State Enumerations, 1782–1785* (Washington: Government Printing Office, 1908), p. 96.
16 The old deeds do not mention "Bacon Hollow" in the boundary descriptions. I have not discovered when the name was first used.

On 20 April 1796, William Morris [48] sold 100 acres of land along Flat Gut Run to William Davis for 30 pounds.

> Beginning on Taylors Creek on the Middle Fork of the run; thence down the same to the fork; thence east to a red oak; thence running east to a chestnut on Flat Gut Run; then up the run to Taylor's line, to the beginning on Flat Top side . . .[17]

This transaction was witnessed by Isaac Davis, Junr., Lewis Davis, Henry Austin, Thomas Barbour, and George Ergentright. One year later, Lewis Davis sold 60 acres of land to Elijah Morris, probable son of William [48].

> . . . tract or parcel of land lying and being in the county of Orange on the Great Mountain Containing by estimation sixty acres be the same more or less and bounded as follows (To Wit) Beginning at a gum water oak and poplar on the branch of the run thence east 20 poles to a hickory, thence north 120 poles to poplar, thence south 20 poles to white oak locust and sycamore on the bank of the run thence down the meanders of the run to the beginning and all the appurtenances . . .[18]

On 10 May 1806, William Morris sent a deed to his presumed son Ika [24]. The content of the deed is lost; only a note mentioning it is extant.[19]

> A deed from William Morris sent to Ika Morris dated the 10th day of May 1806 and which was proved at October Court 1806 by John Shiflett and Jacob Shiflett received by me September 22 1807. Ika (his mark) Morris
> Teste, Richard Chapman

This lost deed was written just two weeks before William Morris [48] transferred ownership of his farm and household possessions to his sons James, Matthew and William, in turn for a promise of care for William, Sr. and his wife in their old age.

> Know all men by these presents, that I William Morris of Orange County, for and in consideration of the natural love and affection which I have to my sons, James Morris, Matthew Morris and William Morris as well as for the further consideration of one dollar to me in hand paid before the ensealing and in delivery of these hereunto, the receipt whereof is hereby acknowledged have given and granted and by these presents as give and grant unto the said James Morris Matthew Morris and William Morris their heirs executors and assigns the following property to wit. All that tract or parcel of land whereon I now live, containing by estimation one hundred and twenty acres more or less lying and being in the county of Orange, and bounded south by Thomas Snow, east by John Davis, north by Elijah Morris and west by Lewis Davis with all and singular the appurtenances thereunto belonging, together with three horses four head of cattle,

---

17 Orange County, Va., Deed Book 21-66, recorded 25 Apr 1796.
18 Orange County, Va., Deed Book 21-195, dated 20 Apr 1797, recorded 24 Apr 1797.
19 Found among a group of "Old Papers of Orange County," microfilmed by the Library of Virginia, reel 561, no page numbers.

seven head of sheep, twenty-six hogs, three feather beds and furniture with every other article of household furniture now in my possession. To have and to hold the said land and property above mentioned unto them the said James Morris Matthew Morris and William Morris their heirs executives administrators and assigns forever: Provided that the said James Morris Matthew Morris and William Morris shall out of the said property above mentioned find their father and mother sufficient maintenance and support during their lives, and the said William Morris, sen. for himself his heirs executors & and the aforesaid tract of land and personal property above mentioned unto the said James Morris Matthew Morris and William Morris their heirs executors & against the claims of him the said William Morris Sen. and against the claim or claims of all and every person or persons whatsoever shall and will warrant and forever ascend: In witness whereof the said William Morris sen. have hereunto set his hand and affixed his seal this 25th day of April 1806.[20]   William (X) Morris

On the Orange County tax lists of 1815, there were a cluster of Morris families living in an area 29 miles west of Orange, the county seat: David, Elijah, Ike, William Morris (Sr.), and William Morris (Jr.).[21] The 1820 census specified only that the male and female heads of the William Morris household were over 45 years of age.[22]

In 1830, the household of William Morris [48] consisted of a man between ages of 70 and 80, and a female between 60 and 70, three women between 20 and 30, and several children.[23] Ten years later (after the area had become Greene County), the census-taker recorded a male between the ages of 70 and 80 in the household of William Morris. A 30-40 year old female and two youth, a boy and a girl between 15 and 20 were there with him.[24]

The dates of death and place of burial for William Morris and his wife are unknown.

---

20 Orange County, Va., Deed Book 24-50, dated 25 Apr 1806, recorded 28 Apr 1806.
21 Roger G. Ward, abstractor, 1815 *Directory of Virginia Landowners (and Gazeteer): Volume 4: Northern Region* (Athens, Ga.: Iberian Publishing Company, 1999), p. 138. Another grouping of Morris families lived east and south of Orange.
22 1820 U.S.census, Orange County, Va., p. 578 written, National Archives micropublication M33, roll 141.
23 1830 U.S. census, Orange County, Va., page 320, National Archives micropublication FM 19, roll 196.
24 1840 U.S. census, Greene County, Va., page 431, National Archives micropublication M704, roll 559.

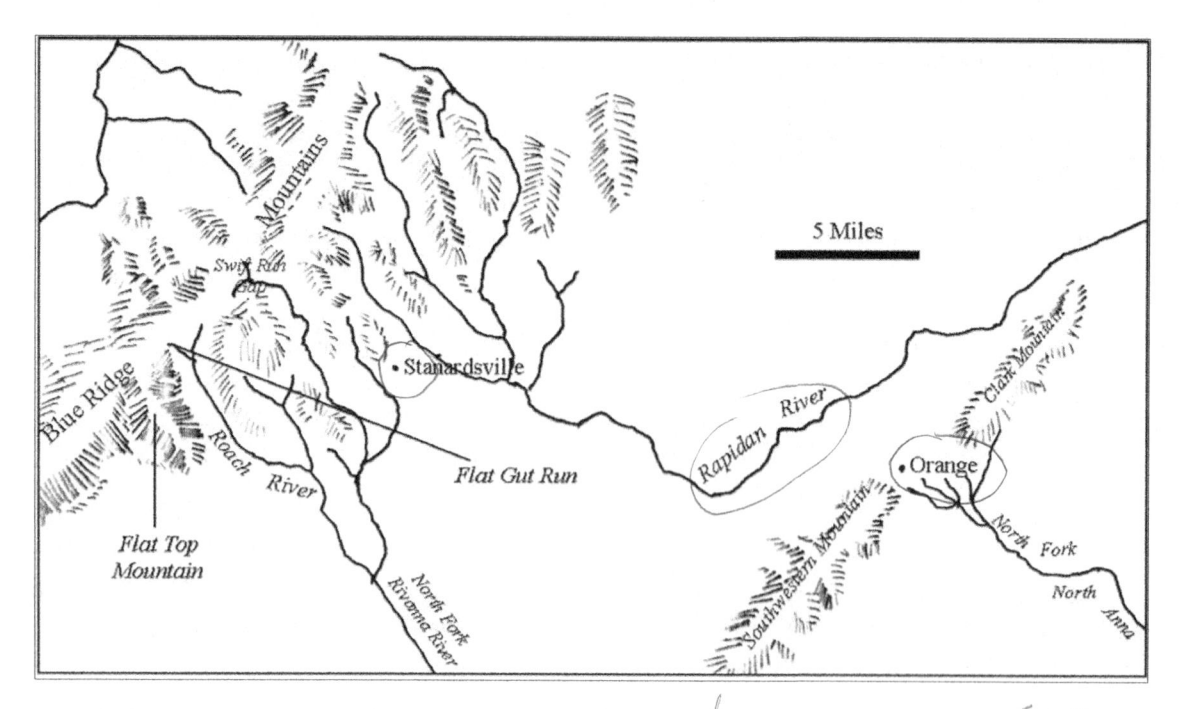

All official business was transacted at the county courthouse. In 1838, the new county of Greene was formed with Stanardsville as its county seat. The residents on the Blue Ridge then had to travel only about 10 miles over the mountains to the courthouse, rather than the earlier 30-mile trek to Orange.

Children of William Morris [48] and ___ ___ [49]

1. Ika [24]　　　　　　　　before 1768 – after 1842　　　　　　m. Elizabeth _____

   b He was of age to sign a deed on 11 May 1789 (Orange County, Va., Deed Book 19-330).

   d He deeded land to his son John on 5 Dec 1842 (Greene County, Va., Deed Book 2-177).

   m Orange County, Va., Deed Book 20-223, dated 23 Sep 1793. "Ika Morris and Elizabeth his wife" were party to a transaction with Lewis Davis.

2. William　　　　　　　　c.1771 – after 1850

   b 1840 U.S. census, Greene County, Va., page 431 (stamped), National Archives micropublication M704, roll 559. Household of William Morris, male 70-80.

   d 1850 U.S. census, Greene County, Va., page 344, dwelling 76, family 76; micropublication M432, reel 947. In household of William Morris, 23, was William Morris, Sr., age 79.

   m Greene County, Va., Death Register, p. 48. A Mary Morris, widow of a William Morris, died at age 90 in March 1877. The name of her parents was unknown. If she was the widow of this William, her name should have appeared on the 1850 census.

3. Elijah   c.1775 – after 1860   m. Elizabeth Geer

   b   1820 U.S.census, Orange County, Va., p. 578 written, National Archives micropublication M33, roll 141. Household of Elijah Morris, male over 45.

   d   1860 U.S. census, Greene County, Va., p. 40 written, dwelling 174, family 174; micropublication M653, roll 1349. Elijah Morris, 84, farmer.

   m   Albemarle County, Va., Marriage Register, 1, 1780–1805, p. 224. The 18 Jan 1802 bond was signed by Elijah and William Morris. Elijah and Elizabeth were married by the minister George Bingham on 9 Feb 1802 (Orange County, Va., Marriage Register No.1, 1757–1867, p. 56).

4. James   1780s – after 1837

   b   1840 U.S. census, Greene County, Va., page 431 (stamped), National Archives micropublication M704, roll 559. Household of James Morris, Sr., male 50-60. The "Sr." is to distinguish him from another younger man of the same name, possibly his nephew, Ika's son. Mentioned in Orange County, Va., Deed Book 24-50, dated 25 Apr 1806. If James were of legal age at that time, he could not be the James Morris, age 66, listed in the 1860 census. Eugene Powell, compiler, *The 1860 Federal Census of Greene County, Virginia* (Quinque, Va.: Compiler, 1998), p. 12.

   d   In an 1837 deed, James Morris conveyed 125 acres to his son Leavy Morris. The tract adjoined Iky Morris (Orange County, Va., Deed Book 36-427, dated and recorded 8 Aug 1837).

   m

5. Mathias (Matthew)   before 1785 – pr. 22 Aug 1836

   b   Mentioned in Orange County, Va., Deed Book 24-50, dated 25 Apr 1806.

   d   Orange County, Va., Will book 8-229, dated 13 Nov 1835. Mathias bequeathed "all my real and personal estate to Lucy Ham for waiting on me in my illness." Executor of the will was his brother James Morris.

   m

6. David   c.1784 – after 1860   m. Patsy Shiflett

   b   1840 U.S. census, Greene County, Va., page 431 (stamped), National Archives micropublication M704, roll 559. David Morris, male 50-60.

   d   U.S. census, Greene County, Va., p. 27, dwelling 206, family 206; micropublication M653, roll 1349. David Morris, 76.

   m   John Vogt and T. William Kethley, Jr., *Orange County Marriages, 1747–1850*, revised edition (Athens, Ga.: Iberian Publishing Company, 1990), p. 87. On 26 Apr 1813, David Morris married Patsy Shiflett, d/o William Shiflett.

7. Polly   m. Shadrack Frazier

   b

   d

   m Orange County Original Marriage Records Book 6-190. 5 Jun 1807. "It is my wish that you should Issue license to Mr. Shadrack Frazier to marry my daughter Polly. Given under my hand this date above written." William (X) Morris. Attested by James (X) Morris and Elisa (X) Morris. They were married on 9 Jun 1807 by the Methodist minister George Bingham (Orange County, Va., Marriage Register No.1, 1757–1867, p 71).

Richard?   before 1778 –   m. Ann ____

   b Richard Morris must of been of legal age to purchase land on Naked Mountain from John and Susanna Shiflet on 24 Apr 1797. Orange County, Va., Deed Book 21-188, recorded 24 Apr 1797.

   d An inventory of a Richard Morris' belongings was taken on 30 Mar 1815. Orange County, Va., Will Book 5-47.

   m Orange County, Va., Deed Book 21-192.

Ika Morris [24]

On 11 May 1789, Ika Morris [24] paid James Taylor £10 for 100 acres of land along Flat Gut Run in the southernmost part of then Orange County.

> This indenture made this 11th day of May anna donime one thousand seven hundred eighty nine, Between James Taylor of Caroline of the one part and Ika Morris of Orange County of the other part witnesseth that this James Taylor for and in consideration of the sum of ten pounds in hand paid the receipt whereof he doth hereby confess and acknowledge hath given granted aliened infeoffed delivered & confirmed and by these presents doth give, grant alien & Deliver and Confirm unto the said Ika Morris his heirs and assigns forever all that Tract or Parcel of Land situate and being in the County aforesaid and bounded as follows. To Wit Beginning at a black Oak & poplar running nearly on southwest course to a water Oak Red Oak near flat gut run, thence up flat gut to Taylors line, thus along under Flat Top and the ledge to Creeds line a south course to the beginning, Containing by Estimation one hundred acres more or less it being part of a larger Tract belonging to the aforesaid James Taylor with all the houses . . .[25]

The signing was witnessed by Hubbard Taylor, Ambrose Madison, and George Taylor, and attested by James Taylor, Clerk of Court.

---

25   Orange County, Va., Deed Book 19-330, recorded 22 Jun 1789.

> James Taylor, an early Virginia immigrant from Carlisle, England, owned a large plantation along the Mattaponi in King and Queen County (later Caroline County). His son, James Taylor II, was one of the landed gentry "Colonels" who accompanied Governor Spotswood on his "Knights of the Golden Horseshoe" expedition to explore the Blue Ridge in 1716. He was one of the first surveyors in Virginia and was responsible for establishing the Hanover, Spotsylvania, and Orange county lines. In 1722, Taylor moved to the area which became Orange County and amassed an estate of 13,500 acres.
>
> The Taylors had obtained headrights for importation of several Morris and Davis men. The names of Taylor descendants pepper the land records of Morris families.
>
> Marshall Wingfield, *A History of Caroline County, Virginia* (1924, reprint, Baltimore: Genealogical Publishing Co., 1969), p. 471. Also, Nugent, Cavaliers and Pioneers, III, pp. 89, 105.

A few years later, Ika Morris and his wife Elizabeth sold half of this land to Lewis Davis for £5.

This Indenture made the twenty third day of Sept. in the year of our Lord one thousand seven hundred and ninety three Between Ika Morris and Elizabeth his wife in the County of Orange of the one part and Lewis Davis of the county aforesaid of the other part. witnesseth that for & in consideration of the sum of five pounds current money of Virginia to him in hand paid . . . Containing by estimation fifty acres more or less . . . Beginning at Creeds line corner to s'd Lewis' Runcold and known by the name of Flatgut thence running up the said run due west 80 poles corner in the above Morris' line to a chestnut and poplar thence running due North 80 poles corner to a chestnut oak thence running due east 80 poles corner to Lewis Davis thence along the said Davis' line to the beginning with all the appurtenances . . .[26]

On 22 Sep 1807, Ika Morris received a deed that his presumed father, William Morris [48] had prepared on 10 May 1806.[27] The content of the deed is lost.

The 1820 census indicates that Ika Morris and his wife were under 45 years of age.[28] (This report is inconsistent with the assumption that he was of legal age in 1789.) In 1830, the census records "Ichabod" Morris, presumably Ika [24], and his three sons James, John and Jeremiah [12] in close proximity. Ichabod's household consisted of a male head between 50 and 60 years of age, two male children under 5, one between 5 and 10, one 10-15, and one male 20-30. Two females were listed: one between 15 and 20, the other 30 to 40.[29]

---

26 Orange County, Va., Deed Book 20-223, recorded 23 Sep 1793.
27 Partly Proved Deeds of Orange County, dated 10 May 1806, proved in the October court. Found among a group of "Old Papers of Orange County," microfilmed by the Library of Virginia, reel #561, no page numbers.
28 1820 U.S.census, Orange County, Va., p. 578 written, National Archives micropublication M33, roll 141.
29 1830 U.S. census, Orange County, Va., page 320, National Archives micropublication FM 19, roll 196.

The name of Ika, Ichabod, or Zechariah Morris is not found in the 1840 census listings. He may have been living with one of the children. The household of his son-in-law, Paschal Morris, included an older male member.[30]

On 15 Mar 1842, for the token consideration of $1.00 each, Ika Morris divided his land and gave 25-acre tracts to three of his children: to James,[31] to Jeremiah [12][32] and to Susanna (married to Paschal Morris).[33] John received his 25 acres on 5 Dec 1842.[34]

No probate records have been found to suggest the dates of death for Ika Morris [24] and his wife Elizabeth ____ [25].

Children of Ika Morris [24] and Elizabeth ____ [25]

1. James   c.1787 – after 1860   m. Sally Morris?

  b 1850 Census, Greene County, Va., page 344, dwelling 91, family 91; micropublication M432, reel 947. James Morris, 53, Sally, 48.

  d James Morris, age 66, is listed in the 1860 census. Eugene Powell, compiler, *The 1860 Federal Census of Greene County, Virginia* (Quinque, Va.: Compiler, 1998), p. 12.

  m A James Morris married Sally Morris on 26 Apr 1814. John Vogt and T. William Kethley, Jr., *Rockingham County Marriages, 1778–1850* (Athens, Ga.: Iberian Publishing Co., 1984), p. 163. However, many researchers feel that James, son of Ika, was the man who had several children with Lucy Ham in the 1820s. Correspondence with Barbara Shifflett Hensley.

2. Susanna   1790s –   m. 1st Slaten Shiflett
                                                                               m. 2nd Paschal Morris

  b 1840 Census, Greene County, Va., p. 432 (stamped), National Archives micropublication 704, reel 559. Household of Paschal Morris, male 60-70, female 40-50.

  d

  m 1st, John Vogt and T. William Kethly, Jr., *Orange County Marriages, 1747–1850* (Athens, Ga.: Iberian Publishing Company, 1990), p. 208. 21 Dec 1818, Susanna Morris, d/o Ikey Morris, m. Slaten Shiflett. 2nd, John Vogt and T. William Kethly, Jr., *Albemarle County Marriages, 1780–1853* (Athens, Ga.: Iberian Publishing Company, 1991), p. 232. 17 Oct 1826, Paskell Morris m. Susan Morris. The father, Zachariah Morriss, who signed his name as Zkey (Ikey?), gave his consent.

---

30 1840 U.S. census, Greene County, Va., page 432 (stamped), National Archives micropublication M704, roll 559. Paschal Morris, one male 30-40, another 60-70.
31 Greene County, Va. Deed Book 2-48, recorded 29 Mar 1842.
32 Greene County, Va., Deed Book 2-49, recorded 29 Mar 1842.
33 Greene County, Va. Deed Book 2-50, recorded 29 Mar 1842.
34 Greene County, Va., Deed Book 2-177, recorded 15 Dec 1842.

3. Jeremiah [12]　　　　　　c.1800 – c.1886　　　　　　m. Peachy Shifflett

    b 1860 U.S. census, Greene County, Virginia, Swift Run District, page 24, dwelling 186, family 186; National Archives micropublication M653, roll 1349. Enumeration date, 18 July 1860. Jeremiah, age 60.

    d The death of a Jerry Morris was recorded on 1 Mar 1885 (Greene County Court House, Register of Deaths, p. 65). However, on 16 Jan 1886 Jeremiah Morris conveyed his farm to his son Burton (Greene County, Va., Deed Book 8-146, recorded 26 Apr 1889).

    m Orange County, Va., Marriage Bonds, 10-291, Minister's Return of George Bingham. On 28 Sep 1824, Jeremiah Morris married Peachy Shifflet, d/o Larkin [26] and Anna Shifflett [27].

4. John ?　　　　　　　　　　　　　　　　　　　　　　　m .Fanny Shiflett

    b

    d

    m Vogt and Kethley, Jr. *Orange County Marriages, p. 88*. A John Morris m. Fanny Shiflett on 13 Apr 1824. There is some question as to whether this was the son of Ika.

Jeremiah Morris [12]

Jeremiah Morris [12] was born about 1800, the son of Ika Morris [24] and Elizabeth ___ [25]. On 28 Sep 1824, he married Peachy Shifflet [13].[35] Peachy was the daughter of Larkin Shiflett [26] and Anna Shiflett [27].

In 1840, the household of Jeremiah Morris was comprised of a man and a woman, both in their 30s, a boy under 5, two boys and a girl between the ages of 5-10, and a boy between the ages of 10 and 15.[36]

It was on 15 Mar 1842 that Jeremiah's father, Ika Morris, conveyed title of 25 acres of his land to Jeremiah.

> This indenture made this 15th day of March one thousand and eight hundred & forty two between Ika Morris of Greene County, Va. of the one part and Jeremiah Morris of said County and State of the other part: Witnesseth that the said Ika Morris, Sr. for and in consideration of the sum of One Dollar lawful money of Va to him in hand paid by the said Jeremiah Morris receipt whereof is hereby acknowledged hath bargained sold and released unto the said Jeremiah Morris his heirs etc. a certain lot or boundary of land lying and being in Greene County suposed to be twenty five acres to be the same more or less and bounded as followeth to wit: Beginning on a mahogany [?] and

---

[35] Orange County, Va., Marriage Bonds, 10-291, Minister's Return of George Bingham.

[36] 1840 U.S. census, Greene County, Va., no. 4 region, page 431 (stamped); National Archives micropublication M704, roll 559.

dogwood some ninety or one hundred Yards below my using Springs and house where I now live, the Mahogany and dogwood stands near set Spring bound eastwards, running thence down the branch say one hundred yds or some distances near that or over cornering on a chestnut ash and Hazlewood north courses, thence running a strait line to Flat Gut run, coming on a chestnut oak and two buttonwood trees on the run, thence up the middle of run to a [?] Spanish Oak in William B. Knight's line, thence running back with Knight's line South courses to a chestnut etc Chestnut Oak, thence with a South course to two Chestnut Oaks, thus running west courses to the beginning: To have and to hold the above named lot and premises free from the claim or claims of all and every person whatsoever that the said Ika Morris do by these presents warrant and defend the right and title to the above named land and premises unto the said Jeremiah Morris and heirs forever. In witness whereof the s'd Ika Morris hath hereunto set his hand and affixed sealed the day and year first above mentioned.[37]   Ika [X] Morris

The 1850 census listed Jeremiah Morris as age 49, a farmer with real estate valued at $150. His wife Peachy was 49; and their children were listed as Richard, 17; Burton, 14; and Hustin, age 11.[38]

Jeremiah Morris bought "50 acres of land, a crop of tobacco and household and kitchen furniture" from William Chapman on 6 Sep 1850.[39] A few months later, on 27 Jan 1851, Jeremiah bought more land. He paid $50 to William Shiflett and his wife Lucretia for a tract of 150 acres adjoining Flat Gut Run, Cold Comfort Cliffs, and land of James Shiflett, William Shifflet, Henry Cook, Eaton, Powell, and Hastin Shifflet.[40]

Jeremiah Morris and Peachy sold 25 acres of land to Haisten Shiflett for $1 on 15 Sep 1853. The land was described simply as "Beginning at a Chestnut Oak and two Bitterwood, thence up the run to a water oak, thence to a chestnut and two Hazlewoods and thence to the beginning."[41]

The census was taken on 18 Jul 1860. Jeremiah was age 60 and Peachy was 61. Their real estate was valued at $75 and their personal estate at $185. Burton [6] was listed as age 20, Huston as 18, and Killis as 14. Their oldest son Sowers, 29, and his wife Artemissa, 26, were living two dwellings away.[42]

All of their children had moved on by 1870. The census recorded Jeremiah Morris, 68, as a farmer. His wife Peachy S. was keeping house. A 14-year-old granddaughter,

---

37 Greene County, Va., Deed Book 2-49, recorded 29 Mar 1842.
38 1850 U.S. census, Greene County, Va., page 17, dwelling 81, family 81; National Archives micropublication 432, roll 947. Enumerated on 8 Aug 1850.
39 Greene County, Va., Deed Book 4-473, recorded 28 Apr 1855. This 1855 deed was an acknowledgment of full payment.
40 Greene County, Va., Deed Book 4-108.
41 Greene County, Va., Deed Book 4-360, recorded 15 Sep 1853.
42 1860 U.S. census, Greene County, Virginia, Swift Run District, page 24, dwelling 186, family 186; National Archives micropublication M653, roll 1349. Enumeration date, 18 July 1860.

Looking across Flat Gut Hollow toward Flat Top Mountain. Flat Gut Run flows between the ridges at the head of Bacon Hollow. Photo taken from the Bacon Hollow Overlook on the Skyline Drive.

Sarah Crawford, was living with them.[43] Ten years later, their reported ages had increased, but not quite ten years: Jeremiah, 77; Peachy, 78; Sarah, 19. Jeremiah was now a retired farmer.[44]

Peachy Shiflett Morris [13] died on 1 Aug 1884 at 85 years of age. Her son Sowers reported to the clerk of court that the cause of death was unknown and that her parents were L. and A. Shiflett.[45]

Six months later, it was recorded that a Jerry Morris, age 80, parents unknown, had died of old age on 1 Mar 1885.[46] However, in a deed dated 16 Jan 1886, Jeremiah Morris sold his 150 acres on the Blue Ridge to his son, Burton Morris, for $100.

---

43 1870 U.S. census, Greene County, Virginia, dwelling 29, family29; National Archives micropublication M593, roll 1649. Enumerated 21 Jun 1870.
44 1880 U.S. census, Greene County, Virginia, Monroe District, enumeration district number 61, page 6, dwelling 50, family 52; National Archives micropublication T9, roll 1468.
45 Greene County Court House, Register of Deaths, p. 21.
46 Greene County Court House, Register of Deaths, p. 65.

Beginning at a sycamore and two Spanish oaks at the foot of Beaver Slide Mountain and running northwest to a forked dogwood and two chestnut oaks, thence with Lydia Shiflett's line, to a double chestnut on Bear slide north, thence northwest with said Lydia Shifflet's line to Mary Shifflet's line thence with the line of William Marsh to a Hickory and two Chestnut oaks, the contested corner in Henry Cook's line, thence northwest with said line to William Eaton's line, thence west with Jeremiah Powell's line to two white oaks in Burton Morris' line, thence south to Hickory on said Morris line, thence N W with said Morris' line to a water oak on a cliff, Catterton's corner and Dr. Sellers, thence south with Catterton's line to a Chestnut [?]on the East side of the mountain, thence S E with Catterton's line to [?] said Catterton's spring, thence south with his line to a double Chestnut thence with said Catterton's line to a slate Rock near the top of the mountain, thence south with Catterton's line to a white oak, Morris corner, thence running south with Brown's line to a Mahogany on the branch, thus running East with Flat Gut Run to the beginning.[47]

It is presumed that Jeremiah Morris [12] died soon after executing this deed. The place of burial for him and for his wife is unknown.

Children of Jeremiah Morris [12] and Peachy Shifflett [13]

1. Sowers　　　　　　　　　　c.1830 –　　　　　　　m. 1st Artamis Shiflett
　　　　　　　　　　　　　　　　　　　　　　　　　　m. 2nd Jane Shiflett

   b *1850 Census of Rockingham County, Virginia*, transcribed by the Harrisonburg-Rockingham Historical Society, from micropublication M432, roll 974 (Athens, Georgia: Iberian Publishing Company, 1997), p. 306. Sowers Morris, 21, Artamisia, 17. 1860 U.S. census, Greene County, Virginia, Swift Run District, page 24, dwelling 188, family 188; National Archives micropublication 653, roll 1349. Sowers Morris, 29, Artemisa, 26.

   d

   m 1st: Eugene D. Powell, *Marriage Records of Greene County, Virginia, 1838–1900* (Quinque, Va.: Compiler, 1998), p. 6. They were married on 10 Aug 1850. 2nd: Shifflett and Hensley, Shiflet, 1700 to 1900, p. 58F. The widower Sowers Morris married the widow Jane Shifflett on 22 Jan 1903.

---

47 Greene County, Va., Deed Book 8-146, dated 16 Jan 1886, recorded 26 Apr 1889.

A Farm on Flat Gut Run 55

2. Richard   c.1833 –   m? 1st Sidney Crawford
                                                                                         m 2nd Fannie Sowers

   b   1850 U.S. census, Greene County, Virginia, page 17 (handwritten at top center), dwelling 81, family 81; National Archives micropublication M432, roll 947. Date 8 Aug 1850. In household of Jeremiah Morris, Richard, 17, laborer. Also, Eugene D. Powell, *The 1860 Federal Census of Greene County, Virginia* (Quinque, Va.: Compiler, 1998), p. 12. Richard Morris, 24, S. A. Morris, 28, and several young Crawford chidren.

   d

   m   No marriage records have been found. Information from Barbara Shifflett Hensley.

3. Burton [6]   5 Aug 1840? – 8 Aug 1930   m. Samantha Frazier

   b   1850 U.S. census, Greene County, Virginia, page 17 (handwritten at top center), dwelling 81, family 81; National Archives micropublication 432, roll 947. Enumeration date, 8 Aug 1850. In the household of Jeremiah Morris, Burton, age 14. 1860 U.S. census, Greene County, Virginia, Swift Run District, page 24, dwelling 186, family 186; National Archives micropublication 653, roll 1349. Enumeration date 18 July 1860. Burton, 20. All later census lists and his marriage registration support an 1840 birthdate.

   d   The Virginia Death Certificate lists his birth date as 5 Aug 1834, making him a grand 96 years old. I suspect that Jeremiah and his family may have exaggerated. Information was provided by his son-in-law, Manuel Morris.

   m   Powell, Greene County Marriages, p. 22. On 31 Dec 1876, Burton Morris, 36, s/o Jeremiah and Peachy Morris, m. Samantha Frazier, 35, d/o Lucinda Frazier. Samantha was born in Rockingham County.

4. Huston   c.1842 –

   b   1860 U.S. census, Greene County, Virginia, Swift Run District, page 24, dwelling 186, family 186; National Archives micropublication 653, roll 1349. Huston, 18.

   d   Presumed buried in the Morris Graveyard on his land on the southwest slope of Flat Top Mountain, above the Simmons Gap Ranger Station.

   m

5. Killis   c.1846 –

   b   1860 U.S. census, Greene County, Virginia, Swift Run District, page 24, dwelling 186, family 186; National Archives micropublication 653, roll 1349. Killis, 14.

   d

   m

> "Where a man having by a woman one or more children, shall afterwards intermarry with such woman, such children, if recognized by him, shall be therefore legitimated."
>
> *The Revised Code of the Laws of Virginia: Being a Collection of All Such Acts of the General Assembly of a Public and Permanent Nature, As are Now in Force* (Richmond: Thomas Ritchie, Printer to the Commonwealth, 1819), I, p. 357.

Burton Morris [6]

Burton Morris [6], the son of Jeremiah Morris [12] and Peachy Shifflett [13], was born about 1840, possibly as early as 1836.[48] When he was in his 20s, Burton established a household with Samantha Frazier, daughter of Lucinda Frazier of Rockingham County. They lived adjacent to his father. In 1870, Burton Morris and Samantha were living together with their children John S., 7; Sarah C., 5; Mary F., 3; and Barbry E., 8 months.[49]

For some unknown reason, despite their commitment to each other and their children, Burton and Samantha had not married. In 1872, Burton signed a deed granting all of his posessions to Samantha.

> This deed made and entered into this 25th day of March 1872 between Burton Morris of the first part and Samanthia Frazier and her bodily heirs of the second part and all of the County of Greene and State of Virginia. Witnesseth that for and in consideration of the Love and affection the party of the first part bears for the party of the second part, the party of the first part doth by these presents, give, grant and convey unto the part of the second part the following property to wit: one black mare (Batz) three cows, five yearlings, seven head of sheep, six head of hogs, one light two horse wagon, one mule (Harry) crippled, Household and kitchen furniture, to have and to hold to her the said Samanthia Frazier and her bodily heirs, as long as she remains unmarried, and in the event of her marrying, then the above named and described property I Burton Morris the above first named party; give unto the now children of the said Samanthia Frazier for their sake and separate use. Witness my hand and seal this day and date first above written.
>
> Burton [X] Morris[50]

Finally, almost five years later, on 31 Dec 1876, conditions were right for the two lovers to marry. According to their marriage record, Burton was then 36 and Samantha was 35.[51]

---

48 The 1850 census lists Burton as age 14. All later records suggest a birth date around 1840.
49 1870 U.S. census, Greene County, Virginia, page 4, dwelling 30, family 30; National Archives micropublication M593, roll 1649. Enumerated 21 June 1870.
50 Greene County, Va., Deed Book 5-559, dated 25 Mar 1872.
51 Eugene D. Powell, compiler, *Marriage Records, Greene County, Virginia, 1838–1900* (Quinque, Va.: compiler, 1998), p. 22.

Burton Morris and Samantha Frazier were married on 31 Dec 1876.

In the census of 1880, Burton Morris is listed as a farmer, age 40. Samantha was listed as "Susan," his wife, age 39, engaged in housekeeping. John S., 18, was a farm laborer. Children in the household were Sarah C., 15; Mary E., 13; Barbara E., 11; William, 9; George E., 7; Ella J., 4; and Emily J., 2.[52] Two more daughters were born to Burton and Samantha: Laura in 1881 and Cecelia or "Cissie" a few years later.

On 11 Nov 1881, Burton purchased 15 acres that adjoined his father's land from Samuel and Victoria Hall. He paid $57 for this "passel of land lying and being in the Counties of Greene and Rockingham in the Blue Ridge."[53] Burton obtained the farm on Flat Gut Run on 16 Jan 1886 when he paid his father $100 cash for 150 acres on the Blue Ridge.[54]

---

52 1880 U.S. census, Greene County, Virginia, Monroe District, Enumeration district number 61, page 6, dwelling 49, family 51; National Archives micropublication T9, roll 1468.
53 Greene County, Va., Deed Book 7-245, recorded 15 Aug 1889.
54 Greene County, Va., Deed Book 8-146, recorded 26 Apr 1889.

In 1900, Burton and Samantha's two youngest daughters were still living with them. Laura was 18, and Sissie was listed in the census as 14.[55] Laura [3] remembered not only the farm work, but also assisting with the still her father operated. In those days before Prohibition, Burton earned cash by making and selling whiskey "to the government."

By 1910, the girls had married. Burton and Samantha continued to engage in general farming with assistance from a grandson, Tom. They owned their home, mortgage free. Neither Burton or Samantha could read or write, but they had managed well in their 70 years.[56] On 20 May 1916, for the consideration of $1, Burton and Samantha Morris deeded a 3-acre piece of their land to their daughter Cissie and her husband, Emanuel Morris.[57]

Samantha died on 16 Mar 1918.[58] The following spring, on 7 Mar 1919, the widower decided to sell his mountain-top farm, all of the 245 acres he had accumulated over the years.

> This deed made and entered into this the 7th day of March 1919, between Burton Morris a widower of the county of Greene and state of Virginia, party of the first part, and E. W. Webster and W. S. Shover of the county of Rockingham, parties of the second part; WITNESSETH: That for and in consideration of the sum of twenty two hundred dollars, fifteen hundred, a part thereof, paid in cash, the receipt whereof is hereby acknowledged, and seven hundred dollars, the balance thereof, evidenced by bond of even date hereof payable on or before the 7th day of March 1920, and bearing interest from date until paid and secured by vendor's lien upon tract of land herein conveyed, the said party of the first part, does grant, bargain, sell and convey, and has by these presents, with general warranty of title. granted, bargained, sold and conveyed, unto the said parties of the second part, jointly all that certain tract or parcel of land lying chiefly in the county of Greene, a small portion thereof lying in the county of Rockingham containing two hundred and forty five acres more or less and bounded as follows, to-wit: Beginning at a chestnut on a path, thence N. 27 W. 128 poles to a double chestnut on a cliff, thence down the mountain, N. 45° W 100 poles to two chestnut oaks, stumps and hickory, "Contested Corner" thence with Burke & Morris line fence (as claimed by both parties) N. 19 ¾ W. 72 poles. thence same course 141 poles a chestnut at the fence Morris and

---

55 1900 U.S. census, Greene County, Virginia, Monroe Township, Enumeratioin District 31, sheet 14, dwelling 229, family 235; National Archives micropublication T623, roll 1711. Enumerated 22 Jun 1900. Burton Morris and Samantha Frazier were married on 31 Dec 1876.

56 1910 U.S. census, Greene County, Virginia, Monroe District,page 20, sheet 4, (dwelling and family numbers are illegible); National Archives micropublication T624, roll 1630. Enumerated April 16, 1910.

57 Greene County, Va., Deed Book 18-243, recorded 1 Oct 1917.

58 On 18 Mar 1918, Burton Morris of Nimrod supplied the information for his wife's death record. The certificate states that she was born on 2 Dec 1838 and died at 79 years, 3 months, and 24 days of age. She was born in Rockingham County, Va., a daughter of Lucinda Frazier and an unknown father. She died at 2 p.m. on 16 Mar 1918 of "heart dropsy." Undertaker E. G. Vernon of Pirkey buried "Samanthy" in the family graveyard. (Commonwealth of Virginia, Registration District 391B, Certificate of Death, File No. 6513. Library of Virginia, microfilm reel 64.)

Burke's corner, S. 30 W 47 poles to two white oaks, thence S. 64½ W. 120 poles, to a spanish oak in a cliff corner to Dr. Sellers, and Catterton, thence with Catterton's line fence S. 5 E. 77½ poles to two chestnuts from one stump, thence S. 33 E. 51 poles, to a bunch of small ash saplings, thence with fence S. 3 E. 32 poles, S. 1 W. 15 poles, S. 33 W. 20½ poles, to a chestnut S. 13½ E. 4 poles, S. 41½ E. 14 poles, S. 25 E. 16 ¾ poles, to a chestnut stump, thence with his fence N. 73 W. 69½ poles, to a stake, thence with his fence, South 20 W. 74 poles, to a white oak, corner to Catterman and Huffman, S 34 E. 33 poles, to a mahogany corner Huffman s## thence with his line fence, S. 16 W. 10 poles, S 17½ W. 18 ¾ poles, S 32½ W. 8 poles, S 25 W. 67 poles, to a mahogany at flat Gut Run, thence down said run 228 poles, to a butterwood corner to Abey Shiflett, thence with his line fence N. 57 W. 5 2/5 poles, N. 17 W. 8 Poles, N. 28½ W. 12 poles, N. 10 W. 6 poles, N. 10 E. 6 poles, N. 17½ E. 6 poles, N. 28 E. 3 2/3 poles, N. 9 E. 2 2/5 to a dogwood, thence N. 34 W. 33 poles to the beginning. These being the lands which were conveyed to the said Burton Morris, by deed from Jeremiah Morris, by his deed dated January 12th 1886, and recorded in the Clerk's office of the circuit court of the county of Greene in Deed Book No. 8 at page 146, and also the land conveyed to said Morris by deed from Sanuel Hall and Victoria Hall by deed dated the 11th day of November 1881, and recorded by the said Clerk's office in Deed Book 7 at page 245, to which reference is hereby made for a further description of said land. To have and hold the said tract of 245 acres of land more or less, unto the said E.W. Webster and W.S. Shover jointly, unto them and their heirs forever. The aforesaid Grantor covenants that he has a right to convey the said land to the aforesaid grantees, that the said grantees shall have quiet possession of the said land, free from all encumbrances, that he has done no act to encumber such land, that he will execute further assurance of said land as may be requisite . . .

However, Burton didn't let go entirely. He reserved the right to cut timber along Flat Gut Run for a period of six years.

There is reserved and excepted from this deed by the grantor all the timber standing, on the East and lower side of a line running from a field below the dwelling house on said land, straight to Flat Gut Run, at or near a crossing, the grantor reserved the right to enter and remove said timber within six years from the date of this deed. All timber not cut and removed from said land within the said period of six years shall at once become the property of the said grantees in this deed, the said grantor shall have the right to build all necessary roads for removal of said timber. Witness the hand and seal of the following party this the day and year first written.

                              Witness John S. Chapman
                              Burton (X) Morris[59]

---

59 Greene County, Va., Deed Book 18-446, recorded 8 Mar 1919.

Following these decisive acts, it seems that Burton began acting like a foolish old man. His granddaughter, Laura's daughter Pearl, bemoaned the fact that "he took up with a woman in Nortonsville and she cleaned him out." Whatever the influence may have been, he overextended himself financially with the purchase of another, larger farm.

On 16 Aug 1919, Burton committed $7,456.30 for the purchase of the 431 acres of the "Old Dunn Tract" near Nortonsville. He paid $2,200.30 cash in hand. But the remaining funds were borrowed. A $1,000 note was due C. E. Gentry. The residue was to be paid in four negotiable notes, each for $1,064.00 at 6% to be paid in one, two, three, and four years.[60]

Immediately, a deed of trust was written naming C. E. Gentry trustee, explaining that the "object of this deed of trust is to secure the payment of said negotiable notes together with all interest to accrue thereon."[61] But Burton could not pay the notes as they came due. Legal process was served against him, and his farm was sold at the courthouse door on 5 Dec 1921.

> . . . Whereas default was made in the payment of several of the debts secured in said deed of trust of August 16, 1919 . . . said property was on this day exposed for sale for cash to the highest bidder in front of the County Court House in Charlottesville, Virginia . . . was knocked out to Emanuel Morris . . . at the price of Three Thousand Seven Hundred Dollars . . . All of that certain tract or parcel of land known as the "Old Dunn Tract," situate, lying and being in the county of Albemarle, the state of Virginia, near Nortonsville, adjoining the lands of C. E. Vie. T. M. Dunn, H. F. Harris, Joseph Smith and others, containing 431 acres . . . being in all respects the said tract or parcel which was conveyed to the said Burton Morris, by J. K. Holman and wife by deed bearing date on August 16, 1919.[62]

Family came to the rescue. The highest bidder at the courthouse sale was Burton's son-in-law, Emanuel Morris, who paid $3,700 for the property. A week later, Emanuel sold 162 acres of the tract to Rias Morris, husband of Barbara Ellen, the daughter of Burton. Rias paid $1,500 to Emanuel, $1,000 of which was "borrowed from Ambrose W. Shifflett and is evidenced by his bond secured by a deed of trust . . ."[63]

Ambrose Shifflett [2] was yet another son-in-law, the husband of Burton's daughter Laura. The loan from Ambrose to Rias was paid in full. A release form is stamped in the margin of the deed book: "The debt $1000 evidenced by the bond herein described and secured, has been paid in full, wherefore the lien of this Deed of trust is hereby released and marked satisfied. Given under my hand the 29th March, 1935."

(Signed) Ambrose W. Shifflett.[64]

---

60 Albemarle County, Va., Deed Book 170-491, recorded 20 Aug 1919.
61 Albemarle County, Va., Deed Book 170-492, recorded 20 Aug 1919.
62 Albemarle County, Va., Deed Book 178-119, recorded 14 Dec 1921.
63 Albemarle County, Va., Deed Book 178-121, dated 12 Dec 1921, recorded 14 Dec 1921. The deed of trust is also dated 12 Dec 1921 (Deed Book 178-124).
64 Albemarle County, Va., Deed Book 178-125.

But had money exchanged hands? Rias' wife died. On 3 Oct 1932, the widower sold his 162 acres of land for $500 to Dewey Shifflett—the oldest son of Ambrose.[65] This was exactly $1,000 less than Rias had paid for the property and exactly the amount borrowed from Ambrose. A family story is that Ambrose loaned the money, Rias couldn't pay it back, and the farm was given to Ambrose. It seems that the farm wasn't "given to Ambrose" but rather that Ambrose arranged for a bargain purchase by his son Dewey. (This farm appears again in a later chapter as a setting for another episode in this saga.)

But what became of the disgruntled old man, Burton Morris? He stayed with his children, first with one, then with another. A grandson, Otto Shifflet, summed it up by saying, "When he got mad at one, he'd move on." Later, a broken hip made it harder to move and to be comfortable or content.

His granddaughter Beulah remembered caring for him. In her memoirs she wrote,

> I also took care of my granddaddy. His name was Burton Morris; we called him Pap. He slept in the kitchen over in the corner. I had to help him in and out of bed, put his clothes on, and carried the night pot to empty. He was on crutches with a broken hip. He could not say Beulah so he called me Julia. He had white hair, white beard, combed his hair with a silver comb, and a little silver comb for his beard. It looked like aluminum. He chewed tobacco, and had some of his teeth when he died at 96. I often think of him now as I get older. Our home was very cold with a fireplace. He would say he was cold and ask me to stoke the fire. I did but sometimes when the wind blew down the chimney the wet wood would not burn.[66]

Burton Morris died on 8 Aug 1930 and was buried in the Morris family cemetery along with his wife Samantha.[67] When "a list of the heirs of the late Burton Morris" was compiled "to be filed with the Clerk of Court as the law directs" on 9 Aug 1930 there were five living children and nine grandchildren listed.[68]

---

65 Albemarle County, Va., Deed Book 217-465, recorded 3 Oct 1932.
66 Beulah Shifflet Herring, *Mountain Memories and Growing Up in the Blue Ridge* (typescript, February, 1990), p. 7.
67 Greene County, Va., Death Certificate. The certificate stated that "Bertram" Morris was born on 5 Aug 1834 and was age 96. This information supplied by his son-in-law Manuel Morris contradicts all earlier census records and his marriage record. I have found that in many cases where a person reaches very old age, the individual and the family tend to exaggerate the number of years.
68 Greene County, Va., Will Book 3-62.

Children of Burton Morris [6] and Samantha Frazier [7]

1. John "Bev"   c.1863 – 28 Jan 1950   m. Frances Crawford

    b   1870 U.S. census, Greene County, Virginia, page 4, dwelling 30, family 30; National Archives micropublication 593, roll 1649. Enumerated 21 June 1870. John S., 7. 1880 U.S. census, Greene County, Virginia, Monroe District, Enumeration district number 61, page 6, dwelling 49, family 51; National Archives micropublication T9, roll 1468. John S., 18, farm laborer.

    d   Obituary, *Greene County Record*, 3 Feb 1950, died "last Saturday," age 87. Buried in Mission Home Cemetery.

    m   Powell, *Greene County Marriages, p. 35*. On 11 Nov 1891, B. Morris, 28, s/o B. & S. Morris, m. F. Crawford, 29, d/o A. & M. Crawford. Bev and "Franky" were living at Sullivan, Virginia on 9 Aug 1930 (Greene County, Va., Will Book 3-62).

2. Sarah Catherine   13 Jan 1865–15 Dec 1939   m. Ahas Shiflett

    b   1870 U.S. census, Greene County, Virginia, page 4, dwelling 30, family 30; National Archives micropublication 593, roll 1649. Enumerated 21 June 1870. Sarah C., 5. 1880 U.S. census, Greene County, Virginia, Monroe District, Enumeration district number 61, page 6, dwelling 49, family 51; National Archives micropublication T9, roll 1468. Sarah C., 15, at home.

    d   Death Certificate, Rockingham County. Buried in Lawson/Wyant Cemetery near Beldor, Va.

    m   Powell, *Greene County Marriages*, p. 32. On 31 Dec 1888, S. C. Morris, 23, d/o B. & S. Morris, m. A. Shiflett, 21, s/o G. & H. J. Shiflett. Ahas and "Dumpling" were living at Island Ford, Virginia on 9 Aug 1930 (Greene County, Va., Will Book 3-62).

3. Mary Frances   7 May 1866 – after 1948   m. Daniel Morris

    b   Census records of 1870 and 1880 suggest she may have been born in 1867.

    d   Buried in the Morris Graveyard, Route 614. Mary F. Morris, 7 May 1866–[blank], also Daniel S. Morris, 24 Feb 1864– 11 Feb 1948. *Greene County, Virginia, Graveyard Survey, 1995–1998*, volume 1 (Stanardsville, Va.: Greene County Historical Society, 1999), p. 99.

    m   Powell, *Greene County Marriages*, p. 29. On 21 Jul 1884, M. Morris, 21, d/o B. & S. Morris, m. D. Morris, 19, s/o S & A Morris. She may have lied about her age to avoid obtaining permission. They were living at Sullivan, Virginia on 9 Aug 1930 (Greene County, Va., Will Book 3-62).

4. Barbara Ellen   c.1869 – between 1921 and 1932   m. Rias Morris

- b 1870 U.S. census, Greene County, Virginia, page 4, dwelling 30, family 30; National Archives micropublication 593, roll 1649. Enumerated 21 June 1870. Barbry E., 8/12. 1880 U.S. census, Greene County, Virginia, Monroe District, Enumeration district number 61, page 6, dwelling 49, family 51; National Archives micropublication T9, roll 1468. Barbara E., 11.
- d Albemarle County, Va., Deed Book 178-124 and Albemarle County, Va., Deed Book 217-465.
- m Greene County, Va., Marriage Register, 1838–1943, p. 49. On 21 Jan 1889, B. E. Morris, 19, d/o B. & S.A. Morris, m. Rias Morris, 19, s/o/ H. & M. Morris. Married by C. H. Biggs.

5. William   1871 – after 1880

- b Census records of Greene County in 1880.
- d Assumed to have died during a typhoid epidemic.
- m

6. George E.   1873 – after 1880

- b Census records of Greene County in 1880.
- d Assumed to have died during a typhoid epidemic.
- m

7. Ella J.   1876 – after 1880

- b Census records of Greene County in 1880.
- d Assumed to have died during a typhoid epidemic.
- m

8. Emily J.   1878 – after 1880

- b Census records of Greene County in 1880.
- d Assumed to have died during a typhoid epidemic.
- m

9. Laura Belle [3]   9 Dec 1881–15 Dec 1973   m. Ambrose W. Shifflett

- b 1900 U.S. census, Greene County, Virginia, Monroe Township, Enumeration District 31, sheet 14, dwelling 229, family 235; National Archives micropublication T623, roll 1711. Enumerated 22 Jun 1900. "Laura M., daughter 18, born Dec 1881." 1920 U.S. census, Rockingham County, Virginia, Stonewall District, Swift Run Precinct, Enumeration District page 99, sheet 6A, dwelling 94, family 96; National Archives micropublication T625, roll 1913. "Ambrose W. Shifflett, rented home, age 46, can read and write, Laura B., wife, age 39, can read, can't write."
- d Buried in the Church of the Brethren Cemetery, Hanoverdale, Pa.
- m Greene County, Va., Marriage Register, 1838–1943, p. 66. On 23 May 1903, Andru W. Shifflett, 27, s/o Evey Shifflett, m. Laura B. Morris, 21, d/o Burton & S. Morris. Married by Killis Roach. They were living at Simmons Gap, Virginia on 9 Aug 1930 (Greene County, Va Will Book 3-62).

10. Cecelia (Cissie)   14 Mar 1883? – 17 Feb 1976   m. Manuel Morris

- b 1900 U.S. census, Greene County, Virginia, Monroe Township, Enumeration District 31, sheet 14, dwelling 229, family 235; National Archives micropublication T623, roll 1711. Enumerated 22 Jun 1900. "Sissie, daughter 14, born May 1886."
- d Buried in the Evergreen Church of the Brethren Cemetery, near Dyke, Va. Ceclia [sic] M. Morris, 14 Mar 1883–17 Feb 1976. Also, Manuel Morris, 11 May 1886–16 Dec 1954.
- m Greene County, Va., Marriage Register, 1838–1943, p. 75. On 3 Apr 1909, Manuel Morris, 22, s/o Smith & Caroline Morris, m. Sissie Morris, 23, d/o Burton & Cymantha Morris. Married by Killis . They were living at Simmons Gap, Virginia on 9 Aug 1930 (Greene County, Va., Will Book 3-62).

The story of Laura Belle Morris [3] who married Ambrose Washington Shifflett [2] is continued on page 99.

Laura Belle Morris, 1881–1973, at age 17.

5 Between the Blue Ridge and Huckleberry Mountain

According to census data of Rockingham County, John Lawson [22] was born in Maryland in 1769.[1] He moved to Virginia as a child or young man. Tax records suggest that he moved into Rockingham County in 1800.[2]

John Lawson and Eva Harnist [23] were married by Rev. John Gibson of Albemarle County on 14 Feb 1803.[3] His bondsman was John Harnist. Michael Harnist and Johannes Harnist were witnesses. Eva was the daughter of Michael Harnist.[4]

Some census data state that she was born in Pennsylvania.[5] The family and given names suggest that she is of Pennsylvania German or Swiss origin, and came to the Shenandoah Valley as the daughter of an early settler. Michael Harnist probably came to Rockingham County in the mid to late 1790s.[6]

John Lawson signed his own name on his marriage bond, evidence of some education. His children and grandchildren growing up on the Blue Ridge would not have that advantage.

John and Eva were listed as between age 26 and 44 in the 1810 census and had two boys and one little girl in their household.[7] Their place of residence in the county is unknown. Perhaps they made their home with Eve's parents. Michael Horness was living at Elk Run in 1815.[8]

---

1 1850 U.S. census, Rockingham County, Virginia, 56 1/2 district, page 188, dwelling 228, family 233; National Archives micropublication 432, roll 974. Enumerated 29 Oct 1850.
2 His name is not on the extant roles of 1793 and 1800, but does appear in 1801 and on subsequent lists.
3 J. Vogt and T. W. Kethley, *Rockingham County Marriages* (Athens, Ga.: Iberian Press, 1984), p. 139.
4 The name is variously spelled as Harnest, Hornest, Harnish, Horness, or Harness.
5 1850 U.S. census, Rockingham County, Virginia, 561/2 district, page 188, dwelling 228, family 233; National Archives micropublication M432, roll 974. The 1870 census states that she was born in Virginia.
6 His name is not on the 1793 tax list but is included from 1800 on.
7 *Index to the 1810 Census of Virgina* (Bountiful, Utah: Accelerated Indexing Systems, Inc.,1978), p. 189. John Lawson, Rockingham County.
8 Roger G. Ward, abstractor, *1815 Directory of Virginia Landowners (and Gazetteer): Volume 4: Northern Region* (Athens, Ga.: Iberian Publishing Company, 1999), p. 162.

I Do Certify the Office of Rockingham County of State of Virginia That have and Do freely Consent to and for licence Between my Daughter Eve Harnest and John Lawson for the State of Matrimony both of the above sd County and State In presence of witness I have here set my seal the Day and Date 1803 February 7th

test
Johannes Harnist   Michael Harnist (Seal)

I Beseech the office of Rockingham County of State of Virginia to grant Licence by the Bearer John Harnist to Solemonize Matrimoney Between my Self and Eve Harnest Both of the above sd County and State Obligem I have here set my hand and seal in presents of witness
test — 1803 February 7th

Johannes Harnist   John Lawson (Seal)

KNOW all men by these presents that we *John Lawson & John Harnest* are held and firmly bound unto *John Page* Esquire, Governor of Virginia, and his successors, for the use of the commonwealth, in the sum of one hundred and fifty dollars, to which payment well and truly to be made, we bind ourselves, our heirs, executors and administrators, jointly and severally, firmly by these presents. Sealed and dated this *11* day of *Febry* 1803

THE condition of the above obligation is such, that whereas a marriage is shortly intended to be solemnized between the above bound *John Lawson and Eve Harnest Daughter of Michael Harnest* of Rockingham County, if therefore, there shall be no lawful cause to obstruct the said marriage, then the above obligation to be void, otherwise to remain in full force and virtue.

Signed, Sealed and delivered in the presence of
John Lawson (Seal)
M A Gambill   Johannes Harnist (Seal)
Sw4 11/5/1940

Consent and Bond for the marriage of John Lawson and Eva Harnest in 1803.

John and Eva continued to live in Rockingham County with their growing family.[9] In February of 1838, John Lawson purchased a tract of land from Joseph Bartlett. Details of the transaction are missing because the deed was one of those destroyed during the Civil War.[10]

However, from later deeds we can surmise that it contained about 120 acres of land on the Blue Ridge mountains near Simmons Gap, lying partly on the east side of Huckleberry Mountain.[11]

The next year, on 28 Apr 1839, Lawson bought an additional 200 acres for $100. This was purchased from "William B. Abbot of the city of Rockingham State of Virginia" and "Luther Billings . . . of Philadelphia state of Pennsylvania." It was located on the mountain on the south side of Powell's Gap and was later referred to as the Baugher tract.[12]

Over the next few years John Lawson accumulated heavy debts. He signed a deed of trust to Samuel Baugher on 1 Apr 1844. This meant that Baugher got title to his 120 acres on the Blue Ridge and Piny Mountains, but Lawson kept the right to use and live on it. The lien was also on "personal property to wit 2 bay mares 3 cows 3 steers 4 Bedsteads and bedding 4 chairs 2 cupboards 1 table 3 sets of cups and saucers 2 dishes 2 sets of knives and forks 1 pot 2 ovens 1 pans 1 skillet 1 kettle 1 shovel & tongs & farming utensils consisting of 2 hoes 2 ploughs 1 levelling knife 1 bigwheel 1 little wheel 1 wheatfan and seives 1 saddle."

> The Union General David Hunter was approaching Harrisonburg on 4 Jun 1864. Fearful that he would follow the policy of burning and destroying public and private property, many of the Court records were loaded on a wagon. The plan was to take them east of the Blue Ridge for safe keeping. However, when a tire came off the back wheel, the wagon broke down on the road leading from Port Republic to Mt. Vernon Forge and Brown's Gap. The teamster unhitched the wagon and left it on the road. Some of Hunter's cavalry found the wagon and records and set fire to them. Mary Keezel who lived nearby, saw it. As soon as the soldiers left, she raked new mown clover from a nearby field and smothered the fire. Water drawn from a nearby well helped extinguish it. Some of the deeds were completely burned and others partially damaged. Nothing left in the courthouse was destroyed. In the 1880s, original deeds and indexes were used in an attempt to reconstruct the burnt deed books.
>
> Mary Nicholas Keezel, *Rescuing the Court Records* (Pamphlet of the Rockingham County Historical Society, 1970), p. 1.

---

9 *Virginia 1830 Census Index* (Bountiful, Utah: Accelerated Indexing Systems, Inc.,1976) p. 162, and Virginia 1840 Census Index (Bountiful, Utah: Accelerated Indexing Systems, Inc.,1978) p. 77.
10 Rockingham County, Va., Burnt Deed Book 12-421. None of this deed could be re-recorded. Another 1844 deed (Burnt Deed Book 19-11) reveals that Joseph Bartlett was living in New York City.
11 Rockingham County, Va., Deed Book 17-481, recorded 19 Apr 1880.
12 Rockingham County, Va. Burnt Deed Book 13-229, recorded 1 May 1839. Re-recorded from the original deed on 18 Nov 1884.

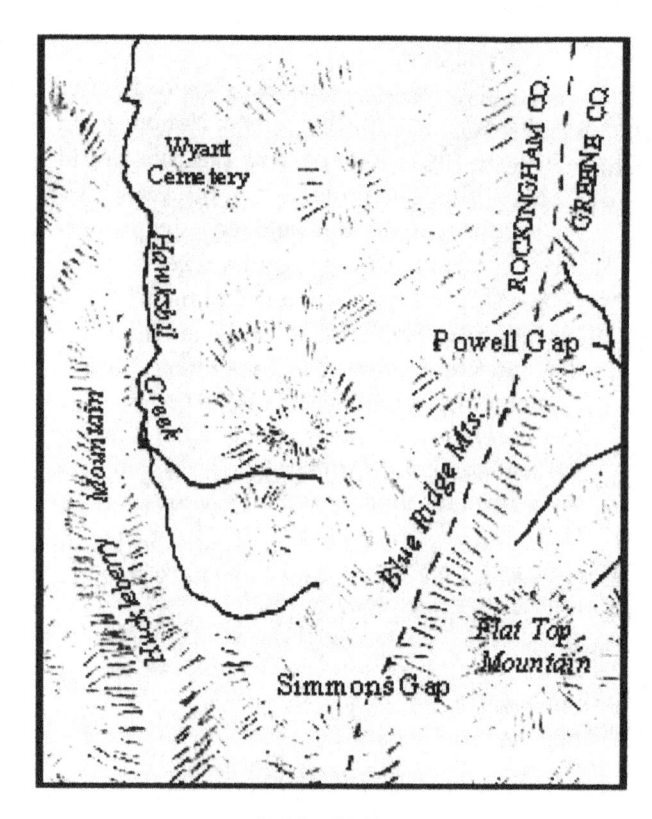

Beldor Hollow

The deed of trust would become void if Lawson paid "Henry Conrad $425 George Baugher $145 the estate of Tobias McGahey $20 Moses Lawson $175 William Marshall $150 Matilda Hufe $200 Theopholis Lawson $200 and Nicholas Shiflet $175 on or before the first day of April 1845." Otherwise all would be sold, with the proceeds used to pay the debts.[13] There is no documentation showing the outcome—but Lawson kept his land.

The census taker who stopped at their home on 29 Oct 1850 listed John Lawson, farmer, as age 81, and his wife Eva, age 64.[14]

John died on 21 Apr 1860. He was buried on his farm. This graveyard, which contains the remains of several generations of Lawson descendants, later became known as the Wyant cemetery.

Eva continued living and working on the farm. At the time of the 28 Aug 1860 census, Eva was age 75, her real estate was valued at $400, and her personal estate at $600. Isaac Wyant, age 23, was living in her household and working as a farm laborer.[15] Another ten years passed, but Eva had slowed her aging! She was listed as age 80 and was keeping house.[16] Eva died in March of 1877, at 91 years af age. She is buried in Wyant's Cemetery beside her husband.[17]

---

13 Rockingham County, Va., Burnt Deed Book 17-142, recorded 2 Apr 1844. This deed survived in entirety.
14 1850 U.S. census, Rockingham County, Virginia, 56 1/2 district, page 188, dwelling 228, family 233; National Archives micropublication M432, roll 974.
15 1860 U.S. census, Rockingham County, Virginia, District No. 1, page 336, dwelling 2436, family 2384; National Archives micropublication M653, roll 1379.
16 1870 U.S. census, Rockingham County, Virginia, Elk Run Township, page 221, dwelling 153, family 153; National Archives micropublication M593, roll 1676.
17 The cemetery is located on the farm of Gordon Wood in the Beldor area, on state Rd. 628. The inscriptions are recorded in "Church and Family Cemeteries of Rockingham County - East of Route 11" (copied by the Massanutten Chapter of the Daughters of the American Revolution, 1965–1971), p. 850.

John Lawson [22], 1769–1860, his wife Eva Harnist [23], 1786–1877, and some of their descendants are buried in the Wyant Cemetery near Beldor. Photos courtesy of Norman Addington.

During his lifetime, John Lawson had sold 75 acres of the Baugher tract to his son Theophilus Lawson. The remaining estate was divided among his heirs.

> Whereas the late John Lawson decd. died Seized of two tracts of land both lying and being in the County of Rockingham and State of Virginia, on the West side of the Blue Ridge. The one known as the George Baugher tract lies partly on the top of said Ridge and the other known as the Bartlet tract adjoining the former lies partly in the East side of whortleberry Mountain. Both containing by recent Survey 437 acres more or less. And whereas the said Lawson at his demise left a widow (who is now dead) and eight children Surviving him . . .[18]

On 12 Jul 1876, Wm. E. Marshall and his wife Malinda sold "all their right, title and interest in the land Estate of the late John Lawson decd lying near Simmons Gap" to Mary Ann Shifflet. She paid $199.31.[19] Matilda Hupp sold her 60-acre share of her father's estate to Mary A. Wood "on or before 8 Apr 1879."[20]

---

18 Rockingham County, Va., Deed Book 17-481, dated 2 Feb 1880, recorded 19 Apr 1880.
19 Rockingham County, Va., Deed Book 25-289, recorded 20 Oct 1884.
20 Rockingham County, Va., Deed Book 25-290, dated 2 Feb 1880.

> The three-tiered plan for elementary and higher education that Thomas Jefferson proposed in 1779 was rejected because of cost. A bill was passed in 1796 that enabled counties to proceed in education as they wished. Most counties wished to do nothing—the rich didn't want additional taxes to pay for education of the poor. The family schools established on prospering plantations became the forerunners of many private schools. Although the University of Virginia was chartered in 1819, the creation of an elementary and secondary school system was postponed. No general education bills could get passed. Education was for the elite few; the majority received no formal schooling.
>
> Matthew Page Andrews, Virginia: *The Old Dominion* (New York: Doubleday, Doran & Company, 1938), p. 357.

Three of those who owned shares—a George Herring, Mary A. Shifflet, and Mary A. Wood—were "anxious to know the particular location" of their interests, and in order to "make a final Settlement and quietus to the matters of dispute concerning each party's interest in said lands," they "mutually agreed among themselves to make Deeds to each other to the land contained in the boundaries." Because each party was "perfectly Satisfied with the boundaries," a comprehensive deed was written on 2 Feb 1880. All of the parties involved signed by making their "X" mark on the deed.[21]

On 14 Dec 1887, Elizabeth Wyant, Rockingham County, Nicholas Herring and his wife Nancy, of Albemarle, and Joseph Lawson, Sr., of Greene County sold to George Herring for $200 their interest in "Two certain tracts or parcels of land of which John Lawson died seized, one known as the Baugher or Home tract of land containing 260 acres more or less . . . and the other known as the Bartlett tract containing 120 acres more or less adjoining the home tract . . ."[22] This deed may have been a formalization of the agreement worked out some years earlier. Mary Ann Shifflett had sold her interest to Charles Davis on 22 Mar 1880.[23]

But all was not settled. On 12 Dec 1888, the heirs were probably surprised to learn that there was pending in the Circuit Court in Harrisonburg "an action of ejectment instituted by The Abbot Iron Company of Baltimore City against sundry parties ncluding the undersigned Theophilus Lawson, George Herring, Charles Davis and Mary Wood the said plaintiff claiming right and title to that large tract or parcel of and lying and being in the counties of Rockingham and Albemarle and Orange, which was granted by the Commonwealth of Virginia to Matthew Gambill by patent bearing date the 8th date of January 1798 and embracing within its boundaries about 219,997 acres of land.

---

21 Rockingham County, Va., Deed Book 17-481, recorded 19 Apr 1880.
22 Rockingham County, Va., Deed Book 36-484, recorded 28 Jan 1890.
23 Rockingham County, Va., Deed Book 10-532, recorded 15 Aug 1881.

Looking toward "Huckleberry" Mountain from the Skyline Drive atop the Blue Ridge today, we can only imagine that the slopes of Beldor Hollow were once valued for their crop lands and the minerals beneath the surface.

And whereas it appears that there lies within the boundaries of said Gambill survey certain lands claimed by said Theophilus Lawson, George Herring, Charles Davis and Mary Wood consisting of a tract of land containing one hundred and twenty acres more or less and being the same tract or parcel of land conveyed to John Lawson by John Bartlett by deed bearing date the 1st day of October 1837."[24]

Apparently, there was not a clear title to the tract bought from Bartlett 50 years earlier. The parties reached a compromise. For $1, the Abbot Iron Company agreed to release rights to the land except for the rights to all "coal, manganese and mineral ores of whatsoever kind deposited or being in" the land.

On 20 Jan 1890, Theophilus Lawson and his wife Margaret Caroline sold all but 33 acres of their land to George Herring for $400.[25] So it was that most of the late John Lawson's property ended up in the hands of George Herring.

---
24 Rockingham County, Va., Deed Book 35-175, dated 12 Dec 1888, recorded 11 Jan 1889.
25 Rockingham County, Va., Deed Book 36-486, recorded 28 Jan 1890.

Who was George Herring? In 1850, George, age 22, was living next door to John Lawson with his mother, Mary Herring, age 45.[26] When George married in 1859 he reported his parents as Loudon and Polly Herring.[27] Polly was a common nickname for Mary. Might "Polly" have been a wife of Loudon Herring, and the same Mary Herring who lived next door to John Lawson in 1850? And might this Mary have been Lawson's daughter? In 1860, only George Herring, his wife and child lived next door to Lawson.[28] This suggests that Mary may have died.[29] When Lawson's estate was settled after Eva's death, it appears that George may have received one of the initial shares. Perhaps Mary was a child that predeceased her father.

The individuals named as heirs in the estate settlement are assumed to be children. Several other persons have been associated with the family, but the available evidence does not clearly establish the relationship. A Marcus Lawson married Rebecca Garver, daughter of David Garver on 7 Oct 1846.[30] Alfred Lawson, who is assumed to be a son, married Francis Wyant on 9 Aug 1834.[31] They had a daughter Lucinda who was married in Rockingham County in 1875.[32] However, it is believed that Alfred may have gone west and died soon after the daughter was born.[33] Marcus, Alfred, and Moses Lawson signed their own names on their wedding bonds or licenses; all others marked with an "X."

Questions also arise concerning the presumed son Moses. Although his name appears on family documents during John Lawson's lifetime, there are no recorded land transactions between Moses and John, and Moses' name does not appear on any of the estate settlement deeds. Most puzzling is that when Moses died, his wife of 37 years said that she didn't know who his parents were![34] John Lawson had died ten years previously, but Eva was still living, relatively close by. Perhaps it was a lazy clerk in the courthouse, perhaps Moses' widow couldn't think under stress, or perhaps he was not a son of John and Eva Lawson.

---

26 1850 U.S. census, Rockingham County, Virginia, 56 1/2 district, page 188, dwelling 227, family 232; National Archives micropublication M432, roll 974. Mary Herring, age 45.

27 Rockingham County, Va., Marriage Bonds and Licenses Book 6-53. A younger Loudon Shifflett, aka Herring, who had moved to Albemarle County, was just a few years older than George. (1850 U.S. census, Albemarle County, Va., p. 185 (stamped), dwelling 415, family 415; National Archives micropublication M432, roll 932. Loudon Shifflett, 29, Lucinda, 25.) This Loudon wrote a will in 1856 in which he referred to his wife Lindy and one daughter. (Albemarle County, Va., Will Book 24-5, dated 26 Jan 1856.)

28 1860 U.S. census, Rockingham County, Va., page 335, dwelling 2452, family 2380; National Archives micropublication M653, roll 1379.

29 Alternatively, she may have been the Mary Herring, 46, who was living in the household of James Morris in 1860. Eugene Powell, compiler, *The 1860 Federal Census of Greene County, Virginia* (Quinque, Va.: Compiler, 1998), p. 12.

30 Rockingham County, Va., Marriage Bonds and Licenses Book 4-765.

31 Rockingham County, Va., Marriage Bonds and Licenses Book 3-1010.

32 Rockingham County, Va., Marriage Licenses, 1865–1889, Part 1, p. 122.

33 Informatiion from Eugene Powell, Quinque, Va.

34 Rockingham County, Va., Register of deaths, 1870–1894, p. 95.

Children of John Lawson [22] and Eva Harnist [23]

1. Moses   c.1805 – 20 Mar 1870   m. Rebecca Baugher

   b 1860 U.S. census, Rockingham County, Va., page 293, dwelling 2119, family 2072; National Archives micropublication M653, roll 1379. Moses Lawson, 54, Rebecca, 52.

   d Rockingham County, Va., Register of Deaths, 1870–1894, p. 95. Died at age 66.

   m Rockingham County, Va., Marriage Bonds and Licenses Book 3-940. 12 Dec 1833. Rebecca was the widow of Isaac Goodall.

2. Elizabeth   1807– 6 Feb 1890   m. David Wyant

   b 1860 U.S. census, Rockingham County, Va., page 290, dwelling 2107, family 2064; National Archives micropublication M653, roll 1379. David Wyant, 55, Elizabeth, 54.

   d Buried in the Wyant Cemetery on Gordon Woods' farm. Elizabeth Wyant, wife of David, died 6 Feb 1890, age 83 years. Also, David Wyant, died 4 Jul 1882, age 76 yrs, 9 mos.

   m Rockingham County, Va., Marriage Bonds and Licenses, Book 3-582. On 18 Nov 1826, David Wyant m. "Elizabeth Lawson daughter of John Lawson." Bond was signed by Moses Lawson.

3. Alfred   d. before 1860   m. Frances Wyant

   b

   d In deeds dealing with the distribution of John Lawson's estate, Alfred is not mentioned.

   m John Vogt and T. William Kethley, Jr., *Rockingham County Marriages, 1778–1850* (Athens, Ga.: Iberian Publishing Company, 1984), p. 139. They were married on 10 Feb 1834 by minister John Gibson.

4. Joseph   26 May 1809 – 27 Feb 1894   m. Selina Snow

   b

   d Buried in the Mitchell Davis Cemetery, Dyke, Va. (Greene County Graveyard Survey (Greene County Historical Society, 1999), p. 97.) Also, Selina Lawson, died 14 Apr 1868.

   m John Vogt and T. William Kethley, Jr., *Orange County Marriages, 1747–1850*, revised edition (Athens, Ga.: Iberian Publishing Company, 1990), p. 236. About 16 May 1835, Joseph Lawson m. Salina Snow, d/o James Snow.

5. Mary Ann [11]   c.1812 – before 26 Mar 1888   m. Kennel Shifflet

   b 1850 U.S. census, Rockingham County, Va., 56 1/2 district, page 189, dwelling 228, family 234; National Archives micropublication M653, roll 974. The household of John Lawson included Mary Shiflet, 38, and several of her children. In 1860 she was listed as 40, as 50 in 1870, and 67 in 1880.

   d Reference to Mary A. Shiflett deceased in Rockingham County, Va., Deed Book 39-119, dated 26 Mar 1888.

   m Rockingham County, Va., Marriage Bonds and Licenses, Book 3-108. "To the Clerk of Rockingham County Virginia. To wit, 1835 February 2nd. I do hereby Certify that Mary Ann Lawson is my daughter and I have given from under my hand for you to grant Licenses for the purpose of Establishing Matrimony between her and Kennelly Shiflett of Orange County of Virginia. In presents witness 1835 February 2nd. (Signed by John Lawson.) Kennel Shiflett and Mary Ann Lawson were married on 22 March 1835 by Rev. John Gibson of Albemarle County.

6. Malinda   c.1817 –   m. William Marshall

   b 1850 U.S. census of Rockingham County, Va., p. 189, family 240: William Marshall, 35, Malinda, 33. *1850 Rockingham County, Virginia, Free Population Census, Slave Census, Mortality Schedule, Social Statistics,* transcribed by the Harrisonburg-Rockingham Historical Society (Athens, Ga.: Iberian Publishing Co., 1997), p. 304.

   d

   m Rockingham County, Va., Marriage Bond & Licenses Book 4-138. (A photocopy of a letter in John Lawson's hand is attached between pages.) 14 Jan 1838. "I do hereby Certify the Clerk of Rockingham County, Va. that have consented and hereby agree for the Clerks of above mentioned County To grant License for purpose of Instituting Matrimony between William Marshall & my Daughter Melinda Lawson of the aforesaid County and State There unto set my hand and seal." Signed by John Lawson and Evy Lawson his wife. Attested by David Wyant.

7. Matilda   – d. after 1880   m. Jacob Hupp

   b

   d Rockingham County, Va., Deed Book 25-290, dated 2 Feb 1880, states that Matilda Hupp is living in Licking County, Ohio.

   m Vogt and Kethley, Rockingham County Marriages, p. 336. They were married on 21 Mar 1838 by minister John Gibson.

8. Nancy   c.1820 –   m. Nicholas Shifflett

   b 1860 U.S. census, Greene County, Va., page 501 (dark crayon), dwelling 178, family 178; National Archives micropublication M653, roll 1349. N. S. Shiflet, 29, Nancy 29.

   d

   m John Vogt and T. William Kethley, Jr., *Albemarle County Marriages, 1780–1853*, 3 volumes (Athens, Ga.: Iberian Publishing Company, 1991), 1, p. 285. About 11 Jan 1843, Nicholas Shiflett m. Nancy Lawson. Later, Nicholas changed his name to Herring. Rockingham County, Va., Deed Book 36-484, dated 14 Dec 1887, refers to "Nicholas Herring and wife Nancy, Albemarle."

9. Theophilus   c.1820 – after Apr 1890   m. Caroline Herring

- b   1850 U.S. census, Rockingham County, Va., 56 1/2 district, page 188B, dwelling 229, family 235; National Archives micropublication M653, roll 974. Theophilus Lawson, 29.

- d   Rockingham County, Va., Deed Book 37-480. 30 Apr 1890. Because they needed money to pay a doctor to cut a swelling from his leg, Theophilus Lawson and wife Caroline deeded their land to their children, retaining their life interest. Ch: Eliza m. Henry Frazier, Amanda m. Samuel Holley, Julia m. Jackson Davis, Delia m. William Coleman, John Lawson, Albert Lawson.

- m   Rockingham County, Va., Marriage Bond & Licenses Book 4-609. 10 Apr 1844. "This is to certify that I am willing for my daughter Caroline Herring to marry Theophilus Lawson, the Clerk of Rockingham County will please to grant license accordingly." Attested by Polly (X) Herring and Kennel (X) Shiflet.

The story of Mary Ann Lawson [11] who married Kennel Shifflett [10] is continued on page 80.

6 What happened to Kennel?

Edward Shiflett [20] was born about 1785–1790. No records have been found that reveal which of the early Shifflets were his parents. The first documentation concerning Edward was his marriage to Joice Herring [21] on 28 Feb 1811 in Orange County. Joice was the daughter of William Herring [42] and Molly Shiflet [43].

James Herring served as bondsman for the couple, granting surety to the clerk of court that the marriage could be held without any legal impediment. Witnesses to the marriage were Charles Parrott and James R. Herring.[1]

From pension applications filed after his death by his widow, we learn that Edward served in the War of 1812. He was drafted into John Miller's Company at the Orange County Courthouse, was engaged in a battle between the United States and the British near Hamilboro, Virginia, and was honorably discharged at Fort Hamilton, Virginia.[2]

The male and female heads of Edward Shiflett's household were classified as between 26 and 44 years of age in the 1820 Orange County census.[3] On 28 Oct 1837, Edward Shiflett and his wife Joice sold a piece of land in Orange County to their son, Nelson Shiflett, who was then living in Albemarle County.[4] This tract adjoined land of Absalom Shiflett. Edward and Joice lived in the area that became Greene County in 1838. In the 1840 census they were classified in the 40-50 age range.[5]

Edward Shiflett died on 20 Feb 1843 in Greene County. The death date was specified in a letter accompanying his widow's pension application.[6] After his death, Joice went to live with their son Henry W. Shiflett. In the 1850 census of Greene County, Joice [21] was listed as 58 years of age.[7]

---

1 J. Vogt and T. Kethley, *Orange County Marriages, 1747–1850* (Athens, Ga.: Iberian Press, 1984), pp. 109, 184.
2 L. F. Shifflett and Barbara Shifflett Hensley, compilers and editors, *Shiflet (and variant spellings) 1700–1900* (Compilers, 1995), p. 27.
3 1820 U.S.census, Orange County, Va., p. 582 written, National Archives micropublication M33, roll 141. I found no Edward Shiflett on the 1830 Orange County census.
4 Greene County, Va., Deed Book 3-76, recorded 28 Oct 1837.
5 1840 U.S. census, Greene County, Va., page 435 (stamped); National Archives micropublication M704, roll 559.
6 Shifflett and Hensley, *Shiflet 1700–1900*, p. 27.
7 1850 U.S. census, Greene County, Va., page 622, dwelling 47, family 47; National Archives micropublication M432, roll 947.

When her son and his family moved to Randolph County, Va., Joice moved with them. They later migrated to Vinton County, Ohio. Joice, who had never remarried, died in Ohio.[8]

Kennel Shifflett [10]

Kennel Shifflett [10] was a son of Edward Shiflett [20] and Joice Herring [21]. He was born about 1810, probably before the 1811 marriage of his parents. His early years were spent in Orange County. He was living there at the time of his 1835 marriage. However, because the bride resided in Rockingham County, the application for a marriage license was submitted in the courthouse at Harrisonburg. The fathers of the bride and of the groom each wrote a request for the license to be granted. Nelson Shiflett, brother of Kennel, signed both requests.[9]

> To the Clerk of Rockingham County of Virginia. to wit 1835 February the 2nd I Do hereby Certify that Kennel Shiflett is my 1st[?] Son and I have giving from under my hand and send for you to grant license for the purpose of Establishing matrimony between him and Mary Ann Lawson of Rockingham County Virginia in present witness. February the 2nd, 1835.
>
>   Nelson Shiplett   Edward Shiplett

> To the Clerk of Rockingham County Virginia. To wit, 1835 February 2nd. I do hereby certify that Mary Ann Lawson is my daughter and I have given from under my hand for you to grant Licenses for the purpose of Establishing Matrimony between her and Kennelly Shiflett of Orange County of Virginia. In presents witness 1835 February 2nd.
>
>   Nelson Shiflett   John Lawson

The Marriage Bond was a printed form on which the specifics were handwritten by the clerk of court.

> Know all men by these presents, that we Kennell Shiflett and Nelson Shifflett are held and firmly bound unto his Excellency Littleton W. Tazewell, Esquire, Governor of Virginia, and his Successors, for the use of the Commonwealth, in the Sum of One Hundred and Fifty Dollars to which payment well and truly to be made, we bind ourselves, our heirs, executors and administrators jointly and severally, firmly by these presents. Sealed and dated this 6th day of March 1835 in the 59th year of the Commonwealth. The Condition of the above obligation is such, that wherein a marriage is shortly intended to be solemnized between the above bound Kennel Shifflett and Mary Ann Lawson Daughter of John Lawson of Rockingham County, if therefore, there shall be no

---

8 Shiflett and Hensley, *Shiflet 1700–1900*, p.27.

9 There is no explanation for the "Shiplett" spellings on the original document. Perhaps another person was asked to pen the letter.

lawful cause to obstruct the said marriage, then the above obligation to be void; otherwise, to remain in full force and virtue.[10]

Kennel (X) Shiflett
Nelson Shifflett

In October 1838, Kennel Shiflett purchased a tract of land in Rockingham County from William B. Abbott. This transaction was listed in an old deed index, but no details are available because the deed itself was among those destroyed during the Civil War.[11] Six months later, Kennel's father-in-law, John Lawson [22], also bought land from William B. Abbott. His tract consisted of 200 acres of mountain land bordering on the south side of Powell's Gap Road.[12] It's likely that Kennel's parcel was nearby.

The procedures for becoming married in the English colony of Virginia were proscribed by law. In 1642, the law stated that "no marriage should be solemnized unless by a license from the Governor or by banns published in their parish."[1] In 1660 it was clarified that if the couple are from two different parishes, the banns must be published in both.[2]

Banns, the announcement of an intended marriage, required the hearers to make known any cause why the parties should not be united in matrimony. Impediments to marriage were lack of free consent, impotency, and legal incapacity due to insanity or minority. The English *Book of Prayer* required that the announcement be made on each of the three Sundays preceding the ceremony. The clergyman could not proceed if there were any objections. For the many early Virginia marriages performed in the church after the proscribed reading of banns, no marriage licenses exist.

The 1705 Assembly spelled out procedures for obtaining a license. "All licenses for marriage shall be issued by the clerk of court of that county where the feme shall have her usual residence." He shall take bond to our sovereign lady the Queen, her heirs and successors, with good surety, the penalty of fifty pounds current money of Virginia, under condition, that there is no lawful cause to obstruct the marriage, for which the license shall be desired, and each clerk failing herein shall forfeit and pay fifty pounds current money of Virginia."[3]

---

1 William Walter Hening, *The Statutes at Large: being a Collection of all the Laws of Virginia,* 13 volumes (1823, reprint, Charlottesville, Va.: University Press of Virginia, 1969), 1, p. 332.
2 Hening, Statutes at Large, 2, p. 50.
3 Hening, Statutes at Large, 3, p. 443.

---

10 Rockingham County, Va., Marriage Bonds and Licenses, Book 3-1083.
11 Rockingham County, Va., Burnt Deed Book 12-507. The index to the "burnt deeds" says that none of this deed remained to be re-recorded.
12 Rockingham County, Va. Burnt Deed Book 13-229, recorded 1 May 1839. Re-recorded from "Original Deed" on 18 Nov 1884.

If either the bride or groom is under 21, he or she must have consent of a parent or guardian. If the clerk doesn't get the signature, he will be imprisoned for one year without bail and fined 500 pounds. The master must give consent for servants to marry. If marrying without consent, the servant must give one additional year of service and pay a fine of 10,000 pounds of tobacco. If a free person marries a servant without consent of his/her master, they must pay the master 1,000 pounds of tobacco. Every October, the clerk of court must send an account of marriage licenses issued that year.[1]

The various fees pertaining to marriage were also proscribed by law in 1705.

to the Governor	20 shillings	or 200 pounds of tobacco
to the Clerk of Court	5 shillings	or 50 pounds of tobacco
to the minister, if by license	20 shillings	or 200 pounds of tobacco
to the minister, if by banns	5 shillings	or 50 pounds of tobacco
for publication of banns	1.5 shillings	or 15 pounds of tobacco

If the groom lived out of county, or was suspected of nonpayment, or was insolvent, the clerk was required to "demand and take bond of every such person or persons, with good security in the county, to pay all fees accruing due . . ."[2]

On the eve of the Revolutionary War, a tax of 40 shillings was levied on every marriage license.[3] Inflation was rampant, and by 1780, the tax for each marriage license was ten pounds. All taxes were to be "paid in the paper money of this state, or of the continent now in circulation."[4] After the war, during a time of adjustments to the new government and currency, the 1792 Laws of the Commonwealth set the fee to the clerk of court for a marriage license, certificate and bond at 87 cents.[5]

With the dissolution of the Established Church, marriage in Virginia became a civil contract. Licensing was official business transacted in the county courthouses. Every license for marriage shall be issued by the clerk of the court of that county or corporation, wherein the feme usually resides, in manner following, that is to say: the clerk shall take bond, with good security, for the sum of one hundred and fifty dollars, payable to the Governor of the Commonwealth, for the time being, and his successors, for the use of the Commonwealth, with condition that there is no lawful cause to obstruct marriage, for which the license shall be desired . . .[6]

---

1 Hening, *Statutes at Large*, 3, pp. 443-445
2 Hening, *Statutes at Large*, 3, p. 445.
3 Hening, *Statutes at Large*, 9, p. 66.
4 Hening, *Statutes at Large*, 10, p. 246.
5 Hening, *Statutes at Large*, 13, p. 390.
6 *The Revised Code of the Laws of Virginia: Being a Collection of All Such Acts of the General Assembly of a Public and Permanent Nature, As are Now in Force* (Richmond: Thomas Ritchie, Printer to the Commonwealth, 1819), I, p. 398.

This conditional bond meant that if the person who gives the bond does some particular act, the obligation shall be void, or else it shall remain in full force. The surety or bondsman was one who guaranteed his performance. If the wedding were not to take place, the surety may be bound to pay the debt. In a time when a 200-acre farm could be purchased for $100, it must have been a daunting act for a man to risk his life savings by signing a friend's marriage bond!

It was not until the middle of the 19th century that the requirement for a $150 bond was dropped. The 1849 Assembly reiterated most of the traditional rules without mentioning a bond.

§1. "Every license for a marriage shall be issued by the clerk of the court of the county or corporation in which the female to be married usually resides, or if the office of clerk be vacant, by the senior justice of such county or corporation, who shall make return thereof to the clerk as soon as there be one.

§2. "Every license so issued shall be registered in a book to be kept by the clerk for that purpose.

§3. "If any person intending to marry be under twenty-one years of age, and has not been previously married, the consent of the father or guardian, or if there be none, of the mother, of such person, shall be given, either personally to the clerk or justice, or in a writing subscribed by a witness, who shall make oath before he clerk or justice that the said writing was signed or acknowledged in his presence by such father, guardian or mother as the case may be."[1]

Reflecting the religious diversity within the state, the laws now specified that "Marriages between persons belonging to any religious society which has no ordained minister, may be solemnized by the persons and in the manner prescribed by and practised in any such society." Fees were also set by law: "Any person authorized to celebrate the rites of marriage shall be paid by the husband a fee of one dollar in each case. Any person exacting a greater fee shall forfeit to the party grieved fifty cents." There was also a $1.00 fee "for a marriage license, for administering and writing certificate of oath, issuing and registering license, and recording and giving receipt for certificate of the marriage."[2]

The license fees were now more reasonable for the average person, but getting married still was not easy for the mountain folks. It required a day-long trip to the county courthouse—and some hopeful effort to find a minister.

---

1 *The Code of Virginia* (Richmond: William F. Ritchie, 1849), p. 469.
2 *The Code of Virginia* (1849), pp. 470, 693

On 28 Jan 1843, Kennel Shifflet conveyed his farm and all of his posessions to trustee William G. Dunn. The deed of trust was written because Kennel was indebted to M. A. Dunkler of Albemarle County for $180.

> This indenture made and entered into this the 28th day of January one thousand eight hundred and forty three Between Kennel Shiflett of the 1st part William G. Dunn of the second part & M A Dunkler of the 3rd part this first named of Rockingham County Virginia the two latter of Albemarle witnesseth that the said Kennel Shiflett to him in [hand purse?] by the said W.G. Dunn the receipt whereof is hereby acknowledged hath granted bargained and sold and by these presents with grant bargain and sell unto the said W.G. Dunn one tract or parcel of land lying and being in the county of Rockingham containing one hundred and fifty acres Adjoining farms Sinnes Esty and others four feather beds four hind cattle one shot gun one loom crop tobucc (com & into) Plantation tools twelve hogs one Bureau one chest two wheels & to have and to hold the said property unto him the said William G. Dunn his heirs and assigns forever free from the claim or claims of all and every person or persons whatever upon the following conditions Whereas the same Kennel Shiflett is justly indebted to M A Dunkl in the sum of one hundred eighty dollars Due by accounts the 1st of January 1843 Now the true meaning and interest of this conveyance is such that should the said Kennel Shiflett will and truly pay the above sum on or before 1st January 1844 then this indenture to be of no further use form or effect whatever but in case failure should occur in part or in whole of what is hereby intended to be paid by the said Kennel Shifflett when at the request of M A Dunns their Exr. the said William G. Dunn is authorized to advertise the above named property at some convenient public place in the neighborhood the time and place being fixed by said Trustee at his own discretion proceed to sell for the highest price that will be given in ready money and after paying the above mentioned as written Debts with interest and costs attending the same the balance if any to be paid to said Kennel Shiflett or his legal representatives. Given from under our hands and seals this day and year last, above written.
>
> William G. Dunn
Kennel (X) Shiflett
M. A. Dunkler[13]

In the Rockingham County court minutes under a list of deeds admitted to record from 1 Jan 1843 to 31 Jan 1843 is "A deed for P estate from Kennel Shiflett to Wm C. Dunn, in trust for M.A. Dunn." Also listed is "A deed for P estate from Edward Shiflett to Wm C. Dunn in trust for M.A. Dunn."[14] Since Edward died on 20 Feb 1843, it appears that Kennel's debt may have been somehow associated with his father's last illness and demise.

---

13 Rockingham County, Va., Burnt Deed Book 16-24, re-recorded from "Original Deed" under Act of Assembly Approval, 18 Nov 1884. This deed was copied in entirety.
14 Rockingham County, Va., Minute Book, 22, p. 8.

What Happened to Kennel?

The next spring, Kennel co-signed a request for a marriage license for Caroline Herring to marry Kennel's brother-in-law, Theophilus Lawson.[15] But after that, there are no more direct records.

What happened to Kennel Shifflett? Did he abandon his family? Did he die? Did he leave the area to search for brighter opportunities? Might he have headed west in the Gold Rush?

An abstract of 1850 land records indicates that Kennel Shiflet owned 150 acres on Lick Run, 18 miles northeast of Harrisonburg.[16] But at the time of the 1850 census enumeration, Mary Ann [11] and the children were living in the household of her parents, John and Eva Lawson. Mary Shiflet was reported as age 38. Her children were listed as Matilda, age 13; Eve, 11; Theophilus, 9; Henry, 7; Mary, 5; and Scott, 3. The census taker erred in recording the ages of two of the children; Theophilus should have been recorded as 11 and Eve as 9 years old.[17]

In 1860, Mary Shifflett, listed now as age 40, was the head of her household and farming. Her real estate was valued at $400 and her personal property at $200. Her sons, Theophilus, age 21, and (Henry) White, age 16, were working as farm laborers. Also in the household were her daughters Matilda, 23; Eva, 19; Mary, 14; Francis, 9; and Jane, 8 years of age.[18]

The census was taken in August. Three months later, on 20 Nov 1860, the children who were old enough to choose a guardian for themselves went to court.

> White Shifflett, Eva Shifflett, Mary Shifflett, children of Kennel Shifflett, being upwards of 14 years of age appeared in court and with the approbation of the court made choice of David Gilmore[19] as their guardian and thereupon the said David Gilmore appeared in court, and together with John S. Hill his security (who justified as to his sufficiency) entered into and acknowledged a bond in the penalty of $400 conditioned as the law requires which bond is ordered to be recorded.[20]

They had no father to serve as guardian. Kennel was either deceased or assumed dead. How long had he been gone? Was Kennel around to father the younger girls? Mary Ann lived adjacent to George Herring and his wife Margaret, and there is suspicion that George may have spent time with Mary Ann.

---

15 Rockingham County, Va., Marriage Bond & licenses Book 4-609.
16 Land Records Abstract, 1850 (typescript at Harrisonburg-Rockingham County Historical Society), p. 45.
17 1850 U.S. census, Rockingham County, Virginia, 561/2 district, page 188, dwelling 228, family 233; National Archives micropublication M432, roll 974. Date 29 Oct 1850.
18 1860 U.S. census, Rockingham County, Virginia, District No. 1, page 335, dwelling 2431, family 379; National Archives micropublication M653, roll 1379. Enumeration date 28 Aug 1860.
19 The abstract of 1850 land records (typescript at the Harrisonburg-Rockingham Historical Society) indicates that David Gilmore owned land along the Shenandoah and in McGaheysville. I have not discovered the reason for him to have been the guardian of choice.
20 Minute Book of Rockingham County, Va., 31-199.

On 22 Feb 1868, Mary Ann and the six older children—Noah, Matilda, Theophilus, White, Eva, and Mary—sold their 150-acre farm to David Gilmore for $200.

> Beginning at a gum tree at the head of the hawksbill thence down the hawksbill to a maple tree on the east side of the hawksbill to John D. Woods corner, thence with John D. Woods line to the top of the mountain to two oak trees cornering with John D. Woods corner, thence along the top of the mountain to two chestnut trees cornering with John D. Woods thence with John D. Woods line to the beginning.

Justice of the Peace, Asa S. Baugher, attested that they all were present and had signed on 8 May 1868.[21]

In 1870, Mary Ann, age 50, was keeping house and had personal property worth $200. She had five daughters living at home. Her brother Theophilus Lawson lived on property adjoining on one side and George Herring lived in the other direction.[22]

After Mary Ann's mother died in 1877, there was impetus to settle the boundary lines of the shares of her father's land. An agreement was prepared in the form of a deed on 2 Feb 1880. Upon payment of one dollar to George and Margaret Herring and one dollar to Mary A. Wood, Mary Ann agreed to relinquish all further rights to their shares of the real estate. They in turn agreed to

> Sell and convey unto the said Mary A. Shifflett all their rights, title, Interest demand and expectancy in that portion of the said Estate containing and included in the following boundary to wit: Beginning at a Gum and Small Chestnut in or near the Wyant line: thence running a dividing between the said Herring and the said Mary A. Shifflet S 30° W 24 poles to a large rock and a Small Poplar on the west edge of said Turnpike;[23] thence N 55° W 14 poles to a Small white oak and two Dog woods on the West edge of said Pike: thence S 27° E 14 poles to a Small Locust on the West edge of an old Road on a hill side: thence S 17 ½ E 8 ½ poles to a Rock planted near a large cherry tree: thence S 17° W 42 poles to a Rock between a Spring and a large Chestnut tree; thence S 37° W 26 poles to a Hickory Sprout and a Rock near Several Cherry trees; thence S 6° W 56 poles to a large Water Oak, a Small Hickory and a Small Spruce Pine on the South bank of the Hawksbill thence S 46° W 11 poles to a Small Gum on the South edge of said stream: thence S 39° W 12 poles to a Sycamore in said Stream and in the line of the old Survey; thence N 45° W 90 poles to a Slate Rock on a a hill side and then Chestnut oak near a large white Pine: thence N 10 ½ W 108 poles to a large Pine and two small ones and a Chestnut Oak in the line of the old Survey and corner to Mary A. Wood; thence with the Division line N 79½ E 128 poles to a Rock on the West edge of said Turnpike near two Hickories thence N 16° W 17 ¼ poles to a small Chestnut Oak on the West edge of said Turnpike: thence S 51° E 54 poles to the beginning; containing 180 Acres more or less.[24]

---

21 Rockingham County, Va., Deed Book 7-78, recorded 3 Feb 1871.
22 1870 U.S. census, Rockingham County, Virginia, Elk Run Township, page 97 (stamped), dwelling 150, family 150; National Archives micropublication M593, roll 1675. Enumerated 16 Jul 1870.
23 The term turnpike was used freely and does not describe the condition of the dirt road.
24 Rockingham County, Va., Deed Book 17-481, recorded 19 Apr 1880.

Almost immediately, Mary Ann sold 26 acres of her land to her son-in-law Charles Davis. He agreed to pay $10 down and an additional $90 in six equal annual payments for

> A certain tract or parcel of land lying in the eastern part of said county on the Hawkbill & Huckleberry Mountain bounded as follows Beginning at a rock and a Persimmon tree in a flat near the house thence South 56° West 102 poles to a Slate Rock on a hillside and three Chestnut Oaks near a large white pine; thence North 10½° W 65 poles to a pine on an old line on a ridge; thence N 80° E 92 poles to three white Oak saplings in a field; thence S 22° E 22 poles to the beginning Containing 26 acres more or less . . .[25]

The census taker in 1880 found Mary A. Shifflet, 67, keeping house. Her daughters, Matilda and Eve, and several grandchildren were living with her.[26]

Mary Ann died in the mid-1880s, sometime before March, 1888. Although there is no marker, it is believed that she was buried in the Wyant cemetery with her parents.

Children of Kennel Shifflet [10] and Mary Ann Lawson [11]

1. Noah Clark   11 Feb 1836 – 4 Jul 1913   m. Virginia Franklin

   b

   d   Buried in Clover Hill Methodist Cemetery, on Rt. 731, off Rt. 613.

   m Rockingham County, Va. Marriage Register. 28 Jul 1870. Noah Shifflett, age 32, single, Rockingham county, s/o Kinley and Mary Shifflett, m. Virginia Franklin, age 23, single, Augusta Co., d/o Jacob and Peggy Andrew. Minister: Jacob Thomas.

2. Matilda   c.1837 –   m. Wm. Nevel Crawford

   b   1850 U.S. census, Rockingham County, Virginia, 56½ district, page 188B, dwelling 228, family 234; National Archives micropublication 432, roll 974. Enumerated 29 Oct 1850. Matilda, 13. In 1860, she was 23.

   d

   m Rockingham County, Va., Deed Book 39-121, dated 10 Jan 1889. The index to the Rockingham County Marriage Register states that Matilda m. William N. Crawford on 29 Dec 1885.

---

25 Rockingham County, Va., Deed Book 10-532, dated 22 Mar 1880, recorded 15 Aug 1881.

26 1880 U.S. census, Rockingham County, Virginia, Stonewall Township, enumeration district No. 74, page 75-76 (stamped), dwelling 553, family 574; National Archives micropublication T9, roll 1388. Enumerated 30 Jun 1880.

3. Theophilus   c.1839 –   m. Columbia Collier

   b 1860 U.S. census, Rockingham County, Virginia, District No. 1, page 335 (stamped), dwelling 2431, family 2379; National Archives micropublication 653, roll 1379. Enumerated 28 Aug 1860. Theophilus, age 21.

   d

   m Eugene D. Powell, *Marriage Records of Greene County, Virginia, 1838–1900* (Quinque, Va.: Compiler, 1998), p. 11. 3 Dec 1863, Theophilus Shiflett, age 22, Rockingham, s/o Kennel and Mary A. Shiflett m. Columbia Collier, age 22, Greene Co., d/o Chapman and Lottie Collier.

4. Eva [5]   11 Jan 1842 – 25 May 1926   unmarried

   b 1860 U.S. census, Rockingham County, Virginia, District No. 1, page 335 (written), dwelling 2431, family 2379; National Archives micropublication 653, roll 1379. Enumerated 28 Aug 1860. Eva, age 19.

   d Death Certificate in the Library of Virginia. Eva died at 84 years, 4 months, and 14 days of age. She is buried in the Lawson/Wyant Cemetery at the home of Gordon Woods near Beldor, Va.

   m Information from her son, Ambrose W. Shifflett.

5. Henry White   c.1844 –   m. E. Margaret Beery

   b 1850 U.S. census, Rockingham County, Virginia, 56½ district, page 188B, dwelling 228, family 234; National Archives micropublication 432, roll 974. Enumerated 29 Oct 1850. Henry, age 7. In 1860, he was listed as age 16. 1870 U.S. census, Rockingham County, Virginia, Stonewall Township, page 33, dwelling 215, family 218; National Archives micropublication M593, roll 1676. White Shiflett, 27, farm laborer; Margaret, 27, keeping house.

   d

   m Rockingham County, Va., Marriage Licenses, Book 1 (1864–1889). 23 April 1867. Henry W. Shiflett, 22 years, 2 months, s/o Kennel and Mary, farmer, married Elizabeth M. Beery, 22, 5 months, d/o George and Sally. Minister: Isaac Long.

6. Mary E.   c.1845 –   unmarried

   b 1850 U.S. census, Rockingham County, Virginia, 56½ district, page 188B, dwelling 228, family 234; National Archives micropublication M432, roll 974. Enumerated 29 Oct 1850. Mary, age 5. 1860 U.S. census, Rockingham County, Virginia, District No. 1, page 335 (stamped), dwelling 2431, family 2379; National Archives micropublication M653, roll 1379. Enumerated 28 Aug 1860. Mary, age 14.

   d

   m Mary was a housekeeper in the home of Thomas Eaton. Her seven children by him were Malinda, Eppa, John, William G., Nancy A., Charles, and William P. (1900 Rockingham County census).

Children of Mary Ann Shifflett [11]

7. Rebecca Frances (Fannie)   c.1851 –   m. Alexander Eaton

   b 1860 U.S. census, Rockingham County, Virginia, District No. 1, page 335 (stamped), dwelling 2431, family 2379; National Archives micropublication M653, roll 1379. Enumerated 28 Aug 1860. Frances, age 9. 1870 U.S. census, Rockingham County, Virginia, Elk Run Township, page 97 (stamped), dwelling 150, family 150; National Archives micropublication M593, roll 1675. Enumerated 16 Jul 1870. Fannie, 18.

   d

   m Rockingham County, Va. Marriage Register. 16 Dec 1871. Alexander Eaton, age 22, single, Rockingham, s/o Benjamin and Gilly, m. Rebecca Francis Shiflett, age 18, Rockingham [no parents listed, line through the space], Married by Washington Carter.

8. Jane   c.1852 –   m. Charles Davis

   b 1860 U.S. census, Rockingham County, Virginia, District No. 1, page 335 (stamped), dwelling 2431, family 2379; National Archives micropublication 653, roll 1379. Enumerated 28 Aug 1860. Jane, age 8. 1870 U.S. census, Rockingham County, Virginia, Elk Run Township, page 97 (stamped), dwelling 150, family 150; National Archives micropublication 593, roll 1675. Enumerated 16 Jul 1870. Jane, 15.

   d

   m Rockingham County, Va. Marriage Register. 19 Oct 1874. Charles Davis, age 22, 7 mo., single, Rockingham Co, s/o ___ and Mary Davis, m. Jane Shifflett, age 23, 2 mo., single, Rockingham Co., d/o Polly Shifflett. Minister: Henry Jones.

After Mary Ann's death, her portion of her father's estate was subdivided into shares for her children. On 26 Mar 1888, Noah Clark Shifflett and his wife Rachel J. Shifflett, of Rockingham sold to Charles Davis for $25, "all of their right, title, interest, expectancy, and demand in and to all the Realty of which Mary A. Shifflet died seized it being a part of the old John Lawson tract of land which consists of the Baugher and Bartlett tracts of land situate, lying and being in the eastern part of the said county of Rockingham on the Blue Ridge 'Huckleberry' Mountain near Simmons Gap, adjoining the lands of Jesse Wyant, George Herring, Mary Wood and others."[27]

The same day, Theophilus Shifflett and Columbia J. Shifflett his wife, living in Page County, sold their share of the estate to their brother-in-law, Alexander Eaton, and released all their rights to the land of Mary A. Shifflett.[28]

---

27 Rockingham County, Va., Deed Book 39-119, recorded 26 Mar 1888.
28 Rockingham County, Va., Deed Book 39-120, recorded 10 Dec 1890.

On 10 Jan 1889, "Alexander Eaton and Rebecca Frances, his wife, Mary E. Shifflett, Henry White Shifflett and Margaret E. Shifflett, his wife, Wiliam Nevel Crawford and Matilda Crawford, his wife, & Eve Shifflett of the county of Rockingham," for $300 paid cash in hand, conveyed all rights to Charles Davis for the "land of which Mary A. Shifflett died seized, and is known as a part of the old John Lawson tract of land, situate . . . on the Blue Ridge and Huckleberry Mountain adjoining the lands of John Wyant, George Herring and others, and contains 150 acres more or less."

Charles Davis thus acquired the entire tract, but the deed specified one important exclusion: "except that the said Eve Shifflett retains her life time interest in the house and lot now occupied by her after which the said house & Lot or garden shall become absolutely and solely the property of the said Charles Davis his heirs and assigns."[29] All eight parties involved signed the 1889 deed by making their mark.

Eva Shifflett [5]

Eva Shifflett [5], usually called Eve, was the daughter of Kennel Shifflet [10] and his wife Mary Ann Lawson [11], born on 11 Jan 1842.[30] The information given to the census takers in later years indicates that Eve was one of those women who got younger as they got older! In 1860, she was 19; ten years later, 23, and in another decade, age 36. Twenty years later, in 1900, she was reported as 44; in 1910, 51; and age 55 in the 1920 census.

Eve grew up in a locality with no schools or churches. All of her education came from life experiences. And living meant hard work in the mountains. The isolated community had little communication with people and events in the mainstream of society. Eve was still a young child when her father disappeared and her mother took the family to live with grandparents. Eve and her brothers helped eke out a living from the mountain farm.

Eve was 19 years old when the Civil War hostilities began and, as a young woman, lived through the ensuing economic turmoil. It was a time of poverty and disintegration of societal values. Family structure among her relatives was in a shambles.

Eve never married. At about the age of 28 she had a child and others followed. At the time of the 1880 census, Eve was living in her mother's household and had a daughter

---

29 Rockingham County, Va., Deed Book 39-121, recorded 10 Dec 1890.
30 On her Rockingham County, Va., Death Certificate, the birthdate and other information was supplied by her son, Ambrose W. Shifflett.

Eve Shifflett about 1870.

Mattie, age 10, and three sons: William J., age 8; Ambrose, 6; and John J., 3 years old.[31] Her daughter Alice was born in about 1884.

Who was the father of these children? The births were not recorded and there are no other contemporary records to substantiate hearsay about the father of three of the children. The marriage records of Eve's two sons, William and John Jonas, indicate that William "Buck" Shifflett was their father. Buck Shifflet was a son of William and Suzanna "Sukey" Shifflet,[32] and the grandson of Richard Shifflet of Albemarle County.[33] Buck Shifflet was a neighbor who lived on the Greene County side of the mountain. He was an older man whose wife died sometime in the 1870s. Might Eve have gone to work as his housekeeper?

It is unfortunate that the 1890 census records were destroyed.[34] There is no way of checking the status of Eve's family for a period of twenty years. The 1900 census lists Eve as head of the household. Living with her were her sons William J., age 27, and Ambrose W., age 24, and her daughter Alice, age 16. Both William and Ambrose were single and working as day laborers. Two grandchildren, William, 6, and James, 5, were also in the household.[35]

When her mother's estate was settled, Eve had been given a lifetime right to continue living in the family home. The wording of the 1889 deed clearly stated that Eve was entitled to the house and garden, but also clearly directed that the property was to be owned by her brother-in-law, Charles Davis, when she gave up the home. In reality, this became an oppressive arrangement. Charles Davis, as folks remember him, was a man with an air of importance. He always was dressed in a suit and tie. He seemed to prefer that others did the work for him. Those others included Eve's sons who worked in Davis' fields.

Alice got married on 20 Dec 1907. Her husband moved in and became head of Eve's household. In the 1910 census records Eve is listed as a mother-in-law of the house painter, Melvin Hansbrough. At that time Alice was 25 and had three children: Otis, 6; Dorothy, 4; and Roy, 15 months.[36]

When Eve's son, Ambrose [2] became caretaker of (and later purchased) a neighboring farm, he moved his mother and his sister's family away from the farm of Charles

---

31 1880 U.S. census, Rockingham County, Virginia, Stonewall Township, enumeration district No. 74, page 346 (stamped), dwelling 553, family 574; National Archives micropublication T9, roll 1388. Enumerated 30 Jun 1880.
32 Greene County, Va., Will Book 1-144, dated 20 Jun 1843.
33 Albemarle County, Va., Will Book 10-42, dated 27 Jan 1827, proved 2 Mar 1830.
34 A January 1921 fire in the Commerce Building in Washington, D.C. destroyed these records.
35 1900 U.S. census, Rockingham County, Virginia, enumeration district 67, Stonewall District, Swift Run Precinct, sheet 1, page 2242, dwelling 6, family 6; National Archives micropublication T623, roll 1726.
36 1910 U.S. census, Rockingham County, Virginia, enumeration district 84, Stonewall Township, Swift Run Precinct, page 1A, line 60, dwelling 13, family 13; National Archives micropublication T624, roll 1627.

Davis to that location.[37] wThe 1920 census also lists Eve as mother-in-law in the household of Melvin Hansbrough.[38] Eve lived with Alice's family on Ambrose's farm for the remainder of her life. She died 25 May 1926 at the age of 84 years, 4 months, and 14 days.[39] She was buried between two of her sisters in the Wyant cemetery where her grandparents and possibly her parents are at rest. Several of Eve's grandchildren later erected a small stone in her honor.

Gravestone in memory of Eve Shifflet.

Eve is remembered as a caring mother and grandmother. She was short in stature, but definitely not frail. Her life was full of hard labor. At the end of a day she relaxed by smoking a corn-cob pipe. Eve and her friends loved to get together and sit around and talk, smoke, and drink coffee. Her son Ambrose, affectionately called "Ammy," had fond memories of being summoned to fetch more tobacco and coffee for his mother.

---

37 The date of the move is uncertain. Alice's son Otis, born in 1903, said it was when he was very young, before he could remember. Ambrose's daughter Pearl, born in 1906, said it was when she was six years old. That would have been the year that Ambrose purchased the farm. See Chapter 7.
38 1920 U.S. census, Rockingham County, Virginia, Stonewall district, Swift Run Precinct, enumeration district 99, Sheet No. 6 (stamped) 301), dwelling 95, family 97; National Archives micropublication T625, roll 1913.
39 Death Record in the Library of Virginia.

Children of Eva Shifflet [5]

1. Mattie E.   c.1869 –   m. Charles E. Shiflett

   b   1880 U.S. census, Rockingham County, Virginia, Stonewall Township, enumeration district No. 74, page 346 (stamped), dwelling 553, family 574; National Archives micropublication T9, roll 1388. Enumerated 30 Jun 1880. Household of Mary A. Shifflet, Mattie, 10, G. Daughter.

   d

   m   Powell, *Greene County Marriages*, p. 34. 29 Nov 1890, C. E. Shiflett, age 21, Greene Co., s/o L. D. and M. Shiflett m. Mattie Shiflett, age 21, Rockingham Co., d/o Eva Shiflett.

2. William John   15 Jul 1871 – 27 Nov 1939   m. Martha Shiflet

   b   1880 U.S. census, Rockingham County, Virginia, Stonewall Township, enumeration district No. 74, page 346 (stamped), dwelling 553, family 574; National Archives micropublication T9, roll 1388. Enumerated 30 Jun 1880. Household of Mary A. Shifflet, William J., 8, G. Son.

   d   Death information from the Death Record in the Library of Virginia, shared by Larry Shifflett. William is buried in Riverview Cemetery, Waynesboro, Va.

   m   Powell, Greene County Marriages, p. 35. 5 Jun 1892, Wm. Shiflett, age 20, Rockingham Co., s/o Wm. and Eva Shiflett m. Martha Shiflett, age 15, Greene Co., d/o Davis and Emma Shiflett. (Photo of Will Shifflett was shared by his grandson, Russell Shifflett of Waynesboro, Va.)

3. Ambrose W. [2]   c.1874 – 14 Oct 1967   m. Laura Morris

   b   1880 U.S. census, Rockingham County, Virginia, Stonewall Township, enumeration district No. 74, page 346 (stamped), dwelling 553, family 574; National Archives micropublication T9, roll 1388. Enumerated 30 Jun 1880. Household of Mary A. Shifflet, Ambrose W., 6, G. Son.

   d   The dates on his tombstone in the Church of the Brethren Cemetery, Hanoverdale, Pa., are 22 Mar 1872–14 Oct 1967. Earlier records suggest he was born around 1874. Also buried at Hanoverdale is his wife, Laura Belle Shifflett, 9 Dec 1881–15 Dec 1973.

   m   Greene County, Va. Marriage Register, 1838–1943, p. 66. 23 May 1903, Andrue W. Shiflett, farmer, age 27, Rockingham County, s/o Evey Shiflett, m. Laura Morris, age 21, Greene Couinty, d/o Burton S. Morris, minister Killis Roach.

4. John Jonas   c.1877 – after 1953   m. 1st Lillie F. Shiflett
                                                                                       m. 2nd May Bell Shiflett

   b   1880 U.S. census, Rockingham County, Virginia, Stonewall Township, enumeration district No. 74, page 346 (stamped), dwelling 553, family 574; National Archives micropublication T9, roll 1388. Enumerated 30 Jun 1880. Household of Mary A. Shifflet, John J., 3, G. Son.

   d   Jonas attended the 50th anniversary celebration of Ambrose and Laura in May of 1953.

   m   1st: Powell, Greene County Marriages, p. 42. 8 Mar 1900, John J. Shiflett, age 22, Rockingham Co., s/o Buck and Eve Shiflett m. Lillie F. Shiflett, age 21, Albemarle Co., d/o ___ and Billie Shiflett 2nd: Greene County Marriage Register, 6 Aug 1918, John Jona Shiflet, age 40, Rockingham County, laborer, s/o William and Evy Shiflett, divorced, m. May Bell Shiflett, age 20, single, Greene County, d/o Larry and Susan Shiflett, minister Killis Roach.

5. Alice   13 Nov 1882? – 29 Oct 1964   m. Melvin Hansbrough

   b

   d   Dates from her tombstone in the family cemetery on Gordon Wood's farm near Beldor. Many earlier sources suggest she was born in 1884. Also in the family cemetery, Melvin Hansbrough, 22 Mar 1886–22 Jul 1965.

   m   Rockingham County Marriage Register. 20 Dec 1907, Melvin Hansbrough, single, age 21, 9 mo., Rockingham Co., painter, s/o M. Jordan and Sarah, m. Alice Shifflett, age 23, single, Rockingham Co., d/o ___ and Eve. Minister: W. L. Wingfield.

Alice and her husband Melvin Hansbrough.

7 On Top of the Mountain

The horrors of the Civil War had ended and Virginia had begun the arduous task of recovery when a second son was born to Eva Shifflett [5]. The exact birthdate of Ambrose Washington Shifflett [2] is uncertain. The family has held that it was on 22 Mar 1872, and that is what is recorded on his tombstone.[1]

Census data present conflicting possibilities. At the time of the 1880 census, Ambrose W, age 6, was living with his mother, sister and brothers in his grandmother's household.[2] In 1900, the census-taker recorded that Ambrose was age 24, and born in October 1875.[3] In 1910, it was recorded that he was 34; in 1920, he was 46 years old.[4] Thus, it appears likely that Ambrose was born later than 1872, probably about 1874.

Ambrose was born and raised in the home of his grandmother, Mary Ann or "Polly" Shifflett. "Ammy" was about 10 years old when his grandma died. His mother, Eva Shifflett, became head of the household.

About the same time, in the fall of 1885, a school opened along the Simmon's Gap

> In 1873, Joseph Baugher and his wife donated one-fourth acre of land near Beldor to the trustees of both the Methodist Episcopal Church of the South and the Church of the United Brethren in Christ with the understanding that "they shall erect and build . . . a place of worship for the use of the members of the above named churches."
>
> Rockingham County, Va., Deed Book 10-434, dated and recorded 13 Dec 1873.

---

1 Church of the Brethren Cemetery, Hanoverdale, Pennsylvania. The birth was not recorded in Rockingham County, Va.
2 1880 U.S. Census, Stonewall Township, Rockingham County, Virginia, page 346 (stamped), dwelling 553, family 574; National Archives micropublication T9, roll 1388.
3 1900 U.S. census, Rockingham County, Virginia, enumeration district 67, Stonewall District, Swift Run Precinct, sheet 1, page 2242, dwelling 6, family 6; National Archives micropublication T623, roll 1726.
4 1910 U.S. census, Rockingham County, Virginia, enumeration district 84, Stonewall District, Swift Run Precinct, page 1A, line 19A, dwelling 4, family 4; National Archives micropublication T624, roll 1647. Enumerated April 15-16, 1910. 1920 U.S. census, Rockingham County, Virginia, Stonewall district, Swift Run Precinct, enumeration district 99, Sheet No. 6 (stamped 301) dwelling 94, family 96; National Archives micropublication T625, roll 1913. Enumerated 13 Jan 1920.

> During Reconstruction after the Civil War, hundreds of schools were established to teach the freed slaves basic reading and writing skills. The Virginia constitution of 1869 finally made provision for planned free schools. Public education for both black and white children was established in 1876. But attendance was not compulsory. Thousands of children didn't bother to go or were put out to work by their parents.
>
> A. Lawrence Kocher and Howard Dearstyne, *Shadows in Silver: A Record of Virginia, 1850–1890* (New York: Scribner's Sons, 1954), p. 198.

road.[5] It is possible that Ambrose Shifflet was one of the first students in the new "Roadside" school.[6] The school was in session only during the winter months. Am learned the basics of reading, writing, and arithmetic in the three years he attended school.

On 10 January 1889, in a final settlement of his grandmother's estate, all of the heirs sold their portions to Am's uncle, Charles Davis. Although Am's mother retained the right to live in the family home during her lifetime, it definitely belonged to Davis. Since education was not compulsory, Am was taken out of school and he went to work for his uncle.

In 1900, Ambrose, age 24, was living in his mother's home, was single and a day laborer. As a first step toward independence, Am acquired a team of mules and a wagon and made his services as a teamster available to the community.

On 28 Jan 1902, an aunt of Howard R. Eiler and Fox D. Eiler gave the two men title to a tract of land "situated part in Rockingham and part in Greene, lying on the East side of the public road crossing Simmons Gap and comprising about 185 acres."[7] Later that year, the Eiler's purchased two additional tracts of adjoining land from R. F. Wyant and his wife Lucy.[8]

> Virginia's railroads were destroyed during the Civil War. As repairs began, there were also dreams of new routes. The Shenandoah Valley railroad company was organized on 23 Feb 1867. The first 42 miles from Hagerstown, Md., to Riverton (near Luray, Va.) opened in December of 1879. In 1880, seventy-nine more miles of track were laid and, on 18 Apr 1881, the railroad was completed to Waynesboro Junction.
>
> Thomas Bruce, *Southwest Virginia and Shenandoah Valley* (Richmond, Va.: J. L. Hill, 1891), p. 208.

---

5 "Roadside School operated 72 years," Elkton, *The Daily Banner,* July 15, 1999, p. 4.
6 An earlier school sponsored by the Methodist and United Brethren Union Church operated from the years 1779–1885. (Correspondence from Dale MacCalister, May, 2000.) Am would have been old enough to attend there. However, this school was probably located near the church, over a half mile farther away from Am's home.
7 Rockingham County, Va., Deed Book 67-144, recorded 3 Feb 1902.
8 Rockingham County, Va., Deed Book 71-110, dated 1 Sep 1902, recorded 8 Oct 1903.

The Roadside School, built in 1885 in Beldor Hollow. The date of this early photo is unknown. Although the school was closed in 1958, the building is still standing and has been renovated by Delbert Wood. Photo courtesy of Casey Billhimer, Elkton.

The Eiler's, who resided in Harrisonburg and Keezleton, had no intention of living on the mountain. They saw the excellent fields of bluegrass as a place to graze cattle—and they needed a caretaker. Ambrose Shifflett, an industrious young man in his 20s, was available. Thus began an amiable working relationship which lasted almost 35 years. Am took care of Eiler's cattle on pasture through the summer. He checked regularly for any problems and laid salt for the cattle on rocks in the fields.

In the fall the cattle would be driven down into the Shenandoah Valley. This informal arrangement, without any exchange of money, was typical of the time.[9] Eiler had the advantage of someone to take care of his land and cattle; Shifflett had the advantage of a home on Eiler's property. It was a one and one-half story, 4-room frame over log house that had been erected about twenty years earlier. In 1903, a small wing was added to enlarge the kitchen, thus making the overall dimensions of the house 14 by 36 feet.[10] The home, located on top of the Blue Ridge nine miles from Elkton, was accessible from the Simmons Gap Road.

With a place to live, Am was in a position to marry his sweetheart and raise a family. On 23 May 1903, Ambrose W. Shifflet [2] married Laura Belle Morris [3]. Laura, the daughter of Burton Morris [6] and Samantha Frazier [7] lived in Bacon Hollow in Greene

---

9 Darwin Lambert, *The Undying Past of Shenandoah National Park* (Boulder, Co.: Roberts Rinehart, 1989), p. 139.
10 Description of H. R. and F. D. Eiler's property, Tract #180, Shenandoah National Park Archives, Box 65, File 20.

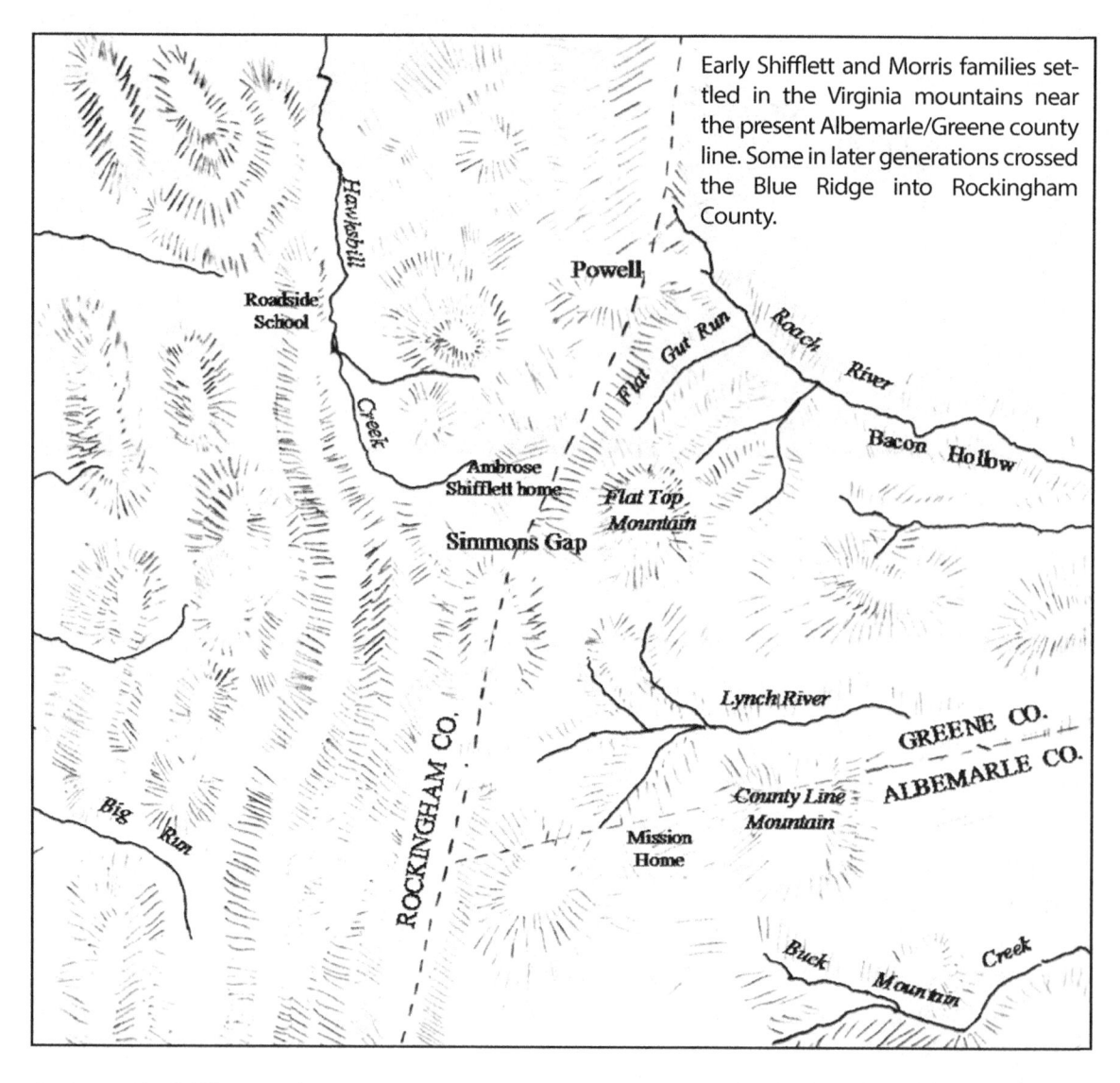

Ambrose W. Shifflett was born in Rockingham County, between Hawksbill Creek and where the Simmons Gap Mission was later built. Ambrose married Laura Morris who was raised in the Flat Gut Run area of Bacon Hollow on the Greene County side of the mountain. They made their home on top of the mountain, about one-half mile from Simmons Gap.

County, on the other side of the mountain. They were married by the minister, Killis Roach,[11] at the home of their friend, Henry Knight.

On 1 Sep 1903 and 18 Nov 1904, the Eiler brothers bought adjoining land from R. F. and Lucy Wyant[12] and Am's responsibilities increased. By 1910, Am and Laura had four children. They lived in the home on land owned by Howard Eiler of Harrisonburg.[13]

In the early years of their marriage, with Laura and the children's help, tending Eiler's cattle was not a full-time job. Am used his wagon and reliable team of mules as a means of earning cash income. He rode deep into the mountains to cut lumber from

---

While the South was recovering from economic devastation, many northern investors saw opportunities. At the intersection of the Chesapeake and Ohio railroad and the new Shenandoah Valley railroad, speculators envisioned a model manufacturing center. A development company was formed on 7 Dec 1889 to build Basic City. They immediately attracted factories and a range of modern businesses. The Normal College from Harrisburg, Pennsylvania, moved there.

A contemporary writer exclaimed exuberantly, "In January, 1890, there was no such place as Basic City in existence, so far as buildings and manufacturing plants go, while in January, 1891, the place has become a town of almost 1,200 people." He predicted, "This place will include Waynesboro within its limits . . . It was the industrial move on the part of this town which caused Waynesboro to wake from its long sleep of country quietude . . ."[1] However, within months, newspapers were commenting on the lull in development in many speculative towns of western Virginia. Many Basic City businesses folded or moved away. When the Normal College building burned in 1892, the college closed forever. The boom had run its course by 1893.

The economy stabilized later in the decade and new businesses were established. W. H. Gardner's Extract Works was operating in 1900. It continued until it was bought out by the Mead Paper Company in 1929. But by then Basic City was a part of Waynesboro. After a vote to consolidate in 1923, the name of the boom town went into oblivion.[2]

---

1 Thomas Bruce, *Southwest Virginia and Shenandoah Valley* (Richmond, Va.: J. L. Hill, 1891), p. 253.
2 Richard K. MacMaster, *Augusta County History, 1865–1950* (Staunton, Va.: Augusta County Historical Society, 1987), pp. 91, 172-173.

---

11 Greene County, Va. Marriage Register, p. 66. 23 May 1903, Andrue W. Shiflett, farmer, age 27, Rockingham County, s/o Evey Shiflett, m. Laura Morris, age 21, Greene County, d/o Burton S.Morris, minister Killis Roach.
12 Rockingham County, Va., Deed Book 71-110, recorded 8 Oct 1903. In 1904, the Eiler brothers bought another 20 acres from George Herring. See Rockingham County, Va., Deed Book 73-494, dated 18 Nov 1904, recorded 21 Nov 1904. The three adjoining tracts contained a total of 102 acres.
13 1910 U.S. census, Rockingham County, Virginia, enumeration district 84, Stonewall District, Swift Run Precinct, page1A, line 19A, dwelling 4, family 4; National Archives micropublication T624, roll 1647. Enumerated April 15-16, 1910.

"government land,"[14] traveling along the ridge to the Big Run area. Am usually took another man, Hosea Shifflett, along to work with him. They would leave their homes on Monday morning with a supply of food, sleep in a shanty during the week, and return home on Saturday evening. Tales are still told of how Am placed rocks in his bunk to make sure he would not oversleep and waste any daylight hours.[15]

They chopped down trees and sawed them into 4- to 5-foot lengths. Loaded into Am's wagon or pulled on skids, the logs were taken to the railroad line at Yancey. There they were loaded onto a railroad car parked on a siding. When the railroad car was full of lumber, Am notified the railroad line and it would be hitched to a train. The logs were delivered down to Basic City and sold to be ground into "extract" for use in making paper. Am was paid $80 for each car full and he tried to ship three carloads each winter.

Much of the cash that Ambrose earned was saved so that he could buy land. On 16 Dec 1912, for $1,800.00, he purchased a 102-acre tract of land from the Eilers. The land was

> . . . lying and being in the eastern part of Rockingham County, Virginia adjoining the lands of Jesse Wyant, Charles Davis and others, and bounded as follows, to-wit: Beginning at a point 6 links N. of white walnut N. 86 E. 118 poles to a Spanish oak, hickory and chestnut; thence S. 24 poles to a stake and pointers; thence N. 78 E. 165 poles to a Spanish oak and fallen hickory in Waterfall Hollow; thence S. 65 W. 165 poles to a double chestnut; thence S. 26 ¾ W. 71 poles to a Spanish oak and hickory, Herring's corner; thence East running with Jesse Wyant's line to a large rock and hickory in Deep Rocky Hollow: thence down Rocky Hollow with H. R. and F. D. Eiler's line to the middle of Simmer's Gap Road; thence with the middle of Simmer's Gap Road; to a large rock and poplar on south side of said road; thence N.E. with Charles Davis' line to within 8 to 10 ft south of a gum; thence N. 47 W. 73 poles to a point in the middle of Simmons Gap Road; thence N. 6¾ W. poles to a turn in Simmons Gap Road; thence N. 24 W. 9 22/25 poles to a point in the middle of said road and corners with Joseph Wood; thence N. 60 E. 55 poles to the beginning: containing 102 acres, more or less . . .[16]

Although he now had his own farm, Ambrose and his family continued to live in the home on Eiler's property. Am had helped his mother and his sister's family move into the house on the "Wyant place," away from their awkward situation on the Charles Davis property. That house was substantial and superior to the one in which

---

14 This would have been part of the Appalachian Division of the Shenandoah National Forest. George Freeman Pollock, *Skyland: the Heart of the Shenandoah National Park* (Chesapeake Book Company, 1960), p. 278.

15 Conversation with Gordon Woods on 15 Jun 2000.

16 Rockingham County, Va., Deed Book 96-58, recorded 31 Dec 1912. Eiler had obtained the acreage from R. F. Wyant, 1 Sep 1903 (Deed Book 71-110), and from George and Margaret Herring, 18 Nov 1904 (Deed Book 73-494).

Am and Laura lived. Laura often felt that Am seemed to care more about his mother and sister than he cared about providing a nice home for his own family.

On the 1920 census records, Ambrose W. Shifflett, age 46, is described as both a renter and a farmer with a grazing farm. His household included his wife Laura B., age 39, and seven children: Dewey, son, 16; Pearle, daughter, 14; Nettie, daughter, 12; Lunzie, son, 10; Edwin, son, 8; Carl, son, 6; and Beulah, daughter, 2 years and 7 months.[17]

There were three more children to come: Otto born in 1920, Edna in 1923, and Kenneth in 1929. A midwife attended the births of the first three children. Later, Doctor Kyger came up the mountain to assist. But for the last child, born when she was 47, Laura went to the hospital in Charlottesville. She stayed there longer than expected when a major snowstorm made it impossible to travel home! A few years later, Laura was back in the hospital. A tumor required the surgical removal of her left eye.

During the 1920s, Ambrose acquired additional parcels of adjoining land from the Wyants.

> This deed, made this 27 day of May 1925 by and between Jesse Wyant and Martha J. Wyant, his wife, parties of the first part, and Ambrose W. Shifflett, party of the second part, all of Rockingham County, Virginia. Witnesseth: That the said parties of the first part, for and in consideration of sixteen hundred dollars cash to them in hand paid by the said Ambrose W. Shifflett, the receipt whereof is hereby acknowledged have bargained, sold and conveyed, with general warranty of title, unto the Ambrose W. Shifflett his heirs, and assigns, all that parcel or tract of land together with the appurtenances thereto belonging situate, lying and being in the eastern part of said county on the Blue Ridge, East of Simmons Gap road adjoining the land of said A.W. Shifflett, William Sellers, T. L. Yancey and others as follows: Beginning at a forked chestnut, near what is known as the Yellow Bank spring and corner to the said A.W. Shifflett's land; thence S. 27 W. 71 poles with the said Shifflett's line to a Red Oak, forming Herring's corner now said A.W. Shifflett's corner; thence, S. 54 E. 154 poles to a point where once stood three hickories and corner to Seller's and Eiler's lands; thence with Seller's line N. 26 ° E. 47 to a corner once known as the Earley's Survey, and a chestnut and a hickory, now probably gone; thence with the same N. 41 E. 195 poles, crossing a branch to a chestnut oak; thence N. 55 E. 60 poles to a large Spanish oak, below the Yancey house, formerly the Powell house thence South Western direction with Several Courses of the Waterfall branch and Yancey's land, formerly the lands of Obediah Crawford and Jerry Powell to a water oak and hickory in said waterfall branch; thence in a straight line in south-western direction with the line of said A. W. Shifflett to the beginning, containing 150 acres more or less to have and to hold unto the said party of the second part forever, and the said parties of the first part covenant to and with the said party of the second part that

---

[17] 1920 U.S. census, Rockingham County, Virginia, Stonewall district, Swift Run Precinct, enumeration district 99, Sheet No. 6 (stamped 301), dwelling 94, family 96; National Archives micropublication T625, roll 1913. Enumerated 13 Jan 1920.

they have the right to convey said land; free from all encumbrances, and that they will make such assurances as may be necessary to protect the title hereby conveyed to the said grantee. The said parties of the first part further agree to allow or give the privilege to the said A.W. Shifflett his heirs and assigns to use the right of way for all purposes as the road or right of way now runs from the above described tract of land beginning at a point near the water oak and hickory corner in waterfall branch, thence through the said home tract of said Jesse Wyant's land as the road now runs to W. W. Coleman's land, thence through the said Coleman's land as the road now runs to R. M. Burke's land, thence through the Burke land as the road now runs to another point in the said Wyant's home tract thence through the Home tract as the road now runs to the Simmons Gap public road, near Alex Shifflett's house. The above mentioned right of way is to be used by the said A.W. Shifflett his heirs and assigns the right of ingress and egress as may be necessary. The said Ambrose Shifflett agrees for himself heirs and assigns that he is to erect a good and substantial gate on the lands of said Jesse Wyant in waterfall hollow, and maintain the same; said gate is near the Coleman house. Also, the said Ambrose Shifflett agree for himself heirs and assigns to make no objection for the land owner of the Jesse Wyant house tract to erect a gate on the said road at or near the "hog fence" now running through the woods to the Water fall creek. The above stipulations shall apply to, not only the said A.W. Shifflett, but his heirs, assigns, and all grantees to where he or they make conveyances of the above mentioned described tract of land. Also, the said A.W.Shifflett his heirs and assigns shall maintain the outside gate, near Alex Shifflett's house. and it is understood, by the said parties to this deed, that the said parties of the first part do not forfeit or surrender any of their rights in and to the above Right of Way given to the said A.W. Shifflett, in the certain deed of record in the clerk's office of said county, in which the several parties conveyed to one another rights of way in and to the road above mentioned. The said parties of the first part agree that the road above mentioned may be widened if necessary, to the width of 12 feet in that part of road above said Coleman's house. The said party of the second part shall have quiet and immediate possession of said land. Witness the following signatures and seals the date first above written.[18]

The next winter, one more parcel of 20 acres purchased from the Wyants completed Ambrose's farm.

This deed made this 27 day of January 1926, by and between Jesse Wyant, Martha J. Wyant, his wife, parties of the first part, and Ambrose W. Shifflett, party of the second part, all parties of Rockingham County, State of Virginia. Witnesseth: That the said parties of the first part, for and in consideration of two hundred fifty dollars ($250.00) cash to them in hand paid by the said Ambrose W. Shifflett, the receipt whereof is hereby acknowledged, have bargained, sold, and conveyed with General Warranty of title, unto the said Ambrose W. Shifflett, all that parcel or tract of land, together with the appurtenances thereto belonging situate, lying and being in the eastern part of said county near the east fork of the Hawksbill Creek, commonly called the "Waterfall Hollow," adjoining

---
18 Rockingham County, Va., Deed Book 132-306, dated 27 May 1925, recorded 8 Jun 1925

the lands of W. W. Sellers, W.W. Coleman, Joe Wood, T. L. Yancey, and the said Ambrose W. Shifflett, and bounded as follows: Beginning at a Spanish oak in the waterfall branch, corner to the said W. W. Seller's, W. Coleman's, T. L. Yancey's and the said Ambrose W. Shifflett's lands; thence with the said Seller's line, West 160 poles to a hickory, corner to Joe Wood's land; thence with his land south 55 poles to a hickory and a White Walnut in the Said Ambrose W. Shifflett's line; thence with his line N. 78 E. 167½ poles to the beginning, containing 20 acres more or less; The said land being the same tract of land conveyed to the said Jesse Wyant by Wm. H. Wyant and wife by deed of date on the 14 day of May 1902 . . .   Jesse Wyant, Martha J. (X) Wyant[19]

These two tracts of land were rich with marketable timber—poplar, locust, hickory, chestnut oak and Spanish oak. In addition to cutting logs for extract, every springtime Am and many of the men in the area earned some cash by peeling bark from chestnut oak and poplar trees. Am carted many loads of bark to Cover's tannery in Elkton. The tannery had been operating since the 1870s and was Elkton's major industry. After an expansion in 1917, when the business was sold in 1918 it was processing 300 hides a day and employed 200 people. As the use of automobiles led to a decreased need for leather tackle, the plant was sold again in 1923 to the Continental Shoe Company. A devastating Sunday morning fire on 15 Dec 1925 destroyed the business. Although a bark extract plant operated briefly in a few remaining buildings, all operations ceased in 1926.[20] The economic impact was felt on the Blue Ridge as well as by the unemployed in Elkton.

Life on their mountain farm was good for Ambrose and Laura, but the endless toil was tedious. The land was steep and rocky. The rocks were picked up and used to build fences. Trees were cut down and brush was cleared. With the children's help, Am planted and tended oats, corn and wheat. The wheat was harvested with scythes. The husked corn was shelled by hand, causing many blisters. Am took the wheat and corn to be ground at Sullivan's mill. From the 56 pounds in a bushel of corn, the miller kept eight pounds for his pay.[21] The flour and meal were necessities for preparing the daily biscuits and cornbread.

> One of the first steps in transforming hides of animals into leather is loosening the hair from the skin. A traditional method was to soak the skins in liquid containing tannic acid. This is obtained from the bark of trees such as oak and hemlock. The chestnut-oak trees of the Appalachian Mountains were an excellent source of tannin extract. The trees were felled and peeled when sap was flowing in the springtime. Sometimes after the bark was sold to a tannery, the logs were sold to a lumber mill or as railroad ties.

---

19 Rockingham County, Va., Deed Book 134-174, dated 27 Jan 1926, recorded 15 Feb 1926.
20 Souvenir Program, Golden Jubilee, 1908–1958, Elkton, Virginia, pp. 32-34.
21 Nettie Shifflett Sullivan, *Mountain Memories* (typescript, undated), p. 8.

Simmons Gap Road in 1900 on the Greene County side of the Blue Ridge. This was the road that Am and his mule traveled to Sullivan's mill.

The photo is from the Frederick W. Neve Papers (#9115). The Albert H. Small Collections Library, University of Virginia Library, and is used by permission.

Ambrose raised cattle, hogs, and sheep. His veterinary skills were valued by the neighbors. The family kept a few cows and chickens to provide milk and eggs. Most of their food was produced on the farm. Vegetables were grown in the large garden and berries were gathered on the mountain. Fruit was harvested from the many apple, peach, and cherry trees in the orchards. Most days, Am would tend to the chores at his home on the Eiler property, then walk part way down the mountain to work on his own farm. The children remember carrying his lunch to him there—the easy walk down, and the slower climb back up the mountain.

In the fall, when the potatoes were dug, Am would load his wagon with potatoes, sweet potatoes, onions, cabbages and chestnuts to sell door-to-door in Harrisonburg. He and his older sons would leave early in the morning for the 25-mile one-way trip.

If they sold out early in the afternoon, they would return home the same day. Otherwise, they would take the horses to a livery stable overnight and sleep in the wagon. Sometimes there was shopping for strips of leather and tacks, necessary for mending harnesses and shoes.

Another cause for a trip to Harrisonburg was the annual necessity of paying the taxes. It would be late at night when Am returned, but for the last few miles he could lay down and sleep. The mules knew their way home.

Am and Laura's home had four rooms, two upstairs and two downstairs. There was a living room with two beds. The parents and the youngest children slept there, while the older boys slept upstairs. Each fall, after the thrashing, the bed ticks would be filled with fresh (and scratchy) straw. The older girls slept in the corner of the kitchen, handy to help with fussy babies and to get up early and start the fire for cooking breakfast.

Ambrose's iron lasts for repairing adult or children's shoes, and the wooden darning shoes Laura used for mending socks.

Near the house was a strong spring. The water ran through a trough in the spring house where the milk and butter were kept cold. Butter was made in a ceramic barrel churn with a wooden plunger. Churning the butter seemed like endless work to the children, especially when it was their responsibility to get the job done while Mom went to town! Laura and her sister "Sis" Morris rode nine miles sidesaddle to Elkton to sell the butter. The cash was used to buy sugar, salt, and coffee.

Laura and the girls had all the women's work to do. The house and porch were swept with brooms that Am made. The living room walls were whitewashed. Clothes were washed with homemade lye soap on a washboard in a big galvanized tub. Before being hung on a line to dry, they were boiled in an iron pot and rinsed in bluing water to make them white. This all-day job was particularly vexing in the winter when it all had to be done indoors.

Laura's father raised sheep and supplied her with wool. After she had thoroughly cleaned and washed it, he would card it and make strips. Laura spent hours spinning wool on her large old-fashioned spinning wheel. Using fine steel needles, she knitted stockings, gloves and scarves for the family. Later, when Am raised sheep, he and Laura sent some of their sheep's wool away to have coverlets woven as a special gift for each of their children.

Five feet tall and even wider, this large spinning wheel was worth its space in Laura Shifflett's home. Wool yarn was essential for knitting warm winter garments. When Laura's sister, "Sis," came over, they enjoyed companionship while the wheel was spinning.

Desiring a sewing machine, Laura shelled walnuts and sold the kernels in Elkton until she had saved enough to purchase a Singer treadle sewing machine. Then she could make the clothing and sew on the patches more easily. She sewed shirts and bib overalls for the boys. From salt and sugar bags she sewed slips and panties for the girls. She constructed quilts and comforts for their beds. But she didn't like making dresses. Much of the girls' clothing was purchased at the "Clothing Bureau," the second-hand store at the Simmons Gap Episcopal mission church.

Cooking, baking, and canning were done on a wood stove in the kitchen. Laura maintained a yeast culture for baking bread. Pies were a regular treat, but without contolled oven temperature in the wood cookstove, Laura was leary of baking cakes.

Frederick W. Neve, 1855–1948. was an English cleric who accepted a call to a parish in Ivy near Charlottesville. Dismayed by the ignorance and superstition he observed on the mountains, and realizing that the children could not be transported to any existing schools, he felt a calling to provide education. In 1900, the first school was opened in Simmons Gap and others followed. Buildings were added to house the teachers and serve as second-hand Clothing Bureaus. In 1911, the Episcopal mission church was consecrated at Simmons Gap.

Frederick W. Neve Papers (#9115), The Albert H. Small Collections Library, University of Virginia Library, Charlottesville, Va.

Nettie and Beulah near their mountain-top home and garden.

Her favorite vegetable was green beans. Throughout the summer there were tender, fresh beans from the vines to be eaten and canned. At the end of the season, the beans were dried and stored for winter. Potatoes and onions were year-round staples. Along with many of the huge cabbages grown in the garden, potatoes, turnips, and apples were nestled in straw and buried in a long trench in the ground for protection from winter's cold.

In the late summer and fall, many long afternoons were spent peeling apples. Then the sliced apples were dried on the roof of the house to be preserved. What a scurry when a thunderstorm came up! Boiling applebutter was a community event. Everybody would help each other peel apples to boil in a 50-gallon copper kettle. Two could stir together and they often sang a song, "Once around the side and twice through the middle."[22]

Much of the family's activity centered around the Episcopal mission at Simmons Gap. The older children began school in the building which had been built in 1900.

---

[22] Beulah Shifflett Herring, *Mountain Memories and Growing Up in the Blue Ridge* (typescript, February, 1990), p. 7

Left: The top of the mountain between Am Shifflett's home and Simmons Gap was not forested in 1931 when Kenneth was a toddler. *Right*: About 1915, Pearl, Nettie, and Lunzie stand on the front porch with Nettie's doll baby. *Below*: Beulah holds the doll, posing with Otto and Edna about 1926.

Sunday morning at the Episcopal mission church at Simmons Gap, Virginia. *Left to right*: Alford Morris (Uncle Bev's son), Stewart Sowers, Ambrose Washington Shifflet, Bev Morris (Laura's brother), John Sullivan.

But, after school attendance became compulsory,[23] they attended Roadside School because their home lay on the Rockingham side of the county line. When the mission church was being constructed in 1910, some of the builders stayed in Ambrose Shifflett's home, paying 25 cents a day for board. Laura appreciated the selection of affordable clothing at the mission's Clothing Bureau. The younger children had fond memories of the women who worked in the mission, particularly Miss Marchant and Miss Comstock. Ambrose and Laura's daughter, Edna, stayed at the Mission Home across the mountain while recuperating from a long illness. The family relied on the telephone at Simmons Gap for emergency contacts.

Every December, the men would go into the woods to gather pine and hemlock for hanging the greens in the church. The women got together to fill small fishnet stockings

---

23 In 1911, Rockingham County was the second county in Virginia to vote for compulsory school attendance. Virginius Dabney, *Virginia: The New Dominion* (New York: Doubleday, 1971), p. 450.

Every Sunday morning Am Shifflett would shave with his straight razor. The imported straight razor, with a carved figure of deer on the ivory handle, would be cleaned and stored again in its case for another week. *Left:* Kenny is dressed for church at Simmons Gap Mission. He remembers falling asleep on the pew beside his mother.

with hard candy. And when all recitations on the Christmas program were spoken, each child was delighted to receive a stocking, an orange, and a gift of a doll or other toy!

On Sundays, the family walked just a short distance from their home to attend worship in the mission church. Frequently, friends would come to their home for Sunday dinner. Sunday afternoons were a time for relaxation. The children enjoyed playing marbles, pitching horseshoes, swinging on a rope swing, or playing checkers on a homemade board.

Friends stopped by frequently to visit throughout the week. When someone arrived at the farm, any hour of the day or night, Ambrose would go to the house and say, "Laura, fix something to eat." She obliged.

Am is remembered as an easy-going daddy, a kind man, and a good, helpful neighbor. He loved to help people. He carried baskets of food to families experiencing hard times. He helped people pay for their homes. He loaned money to friends in need, even though there was slight chance of being repaid.

Laura assumed the role of disciplinarian. When she felt that punishment was need-

About 1933, big sister Pearl *(center back)* is home for a visit. With Huckleberry Mountain in the background, the family poses along the road from their home to Simmons Gap. *Left to right*: Carl, Beulah, Edna, Otto, Ambrose and Laura, with Kenneth standing in front of his parents.

ed—which, in the children's memory, was often—she instructed the offender to go out and cut a switch. They had to bring it in and endure both the psychological punishment of dread and the physical pain of the switching.

By the time the younger children came along, some of the older ones had gone from home to work and to marry. Am sent each of the boys on their way with a new suit and $100. For the younger ones, it was exciting when an older sibling would come home for a visit, driving a car and telling tales of life and work at the chocolate factory in Hershey, Pennsylvania.

But Ambrose and Laura were content. They expected to spend their twilight years watching the beautiful mountain sunsets from their front porch.

8 Ambrose and the Exodus

When Ambrose Shifflett purchased the final portion of his mountain farm in January of 1926, he probably did not realize that plans were already being laid that could take it away from him. They weren't designs of a neighbor coveting his timber. They were dreams of a society, influenced by a changing world.

Ambrose and Laura were living in the early years of the 20th century, at a time in which Americans placed great faith in science and new discoveries. Science provided the basis for new laws regulating sanitation, meat packing, and urban water supplies. Improved hospitals and medical practices were the product of science. Technological advances revolutionized transportation and communication. Scientific surveys documented the systematic nature of social problems. Through the application of scientific principles, the conditions of human lives could be improved.

With the efforts of enlightened people, the world could become a better place! Many people came to believe that they knew what was best for other people. For example, it was considered best for Native Americans to be assimilated into the predominant culture. If the children were educated in boarding schools, away from their families and tribal traditions, they would quickly become true Americans.

Well-meaning Christian missionaries traveled to foreign lands, teaching the indigenous people to work and worship the American way. In the growing field of social work, "friendly visitors" studied the plight of poor families and decided upon appropriate interventions. Many believed that poverty could be eradicated by intervention or treatment and that the poor would be morally elevated by the role model of the caseworkers.

There was a growing belief that government could be an instrument for improvement. Legislation prohibiting the sale of liquor was expected to solve the problems caused by alcoholism and drunkenness. The plight of children was studied and child labor laws were debated. Concern for the many children being sent to orphanages prompted enactment of laws governing widows' pensions. The field of social work widened to include medical and psychiatric practitioners with an emphasis on helping "disorganized" families. Americans truly believed that, collectively, they could become better and better each day.

Idealists said that World War I was fought to make the world safe for democracy. However, the aftermath of the war bred a nationalistic, alien-hating element in the United States. Although the revived Ku Klux Klan never got much of a foothold in Virginia,[1] the nation was ripe for its propaganda, and membership reached a peak of between four and five million by 1925. The declared purpose of the Ku-Klux Klan was to maintain "all that is chivalric in conduct, noble in sentiment, generous in manhood, and patriotic in purpose." They denounced "Negroes, bootleggers, adulterers, Jews, Pacifists, radicals, Catholics, evolutionists, and other persons who did not conform in race or ideas to what the Klansmen considered proper standards of Americanism." [2]

Racial integrity became an obsession among many in prominent positions. Walter A. Plecker, who in 1912 became the first registrar of the Virginia Bureau of Vital Statistics, believed that many with mixed racial background were trying to pass as white. Fines were imposed on doctors and midwives who did not report this. Pen in hand, Plecker himself "corrected" the birth certificates of some individuals. In 1943 he sent a list of suspect surnames to all county health officials—Shiflett was on the long list.

Although involuntary sterilization has been associated with Nazi Germany, the eugenics movement had a strong component in the United States. In fact, the German law was modeled on a 1924 Virginia law endorsed by Plecker! Society may have pitied, but had little tolerance for individuals deemed inferior by an accident of birth.

Feeble-mindedness, criminal behavior, epilepsy, alcoholism and immorality were believed to be heritable. When a parent or the community deemed there was a problem, a judge or social worker could diagnose individuals, declare them a misfit, and have them institutionalized and at risk for sterilization. The stated purpose of sterilization was to prevent the birth of defectives, thus safeguarding every child's birthright to a sound mind in a sound body.[3]

The eugenists, the social workers, the Ku-Klux Klan, the public health workers, the educators, the Prohibitionist, and the man-on-the-street only wanted what was best for America—each defining the best from his own perspective.

And America did get "better" as telephones, plumbing, electricity, safer food and water, education, and automobiles came into the lives of the people. A chasm grew between those who could enjoy the modern amenities and those, such as the families living on the Blue Ridge, who did not have access to such conveniences. The mountain folk continued to live and work in their traditional ways, more or less isolated from the changing society. Practical experience and superstition, not formal education, determined behavior.

---
[1] Virginius Dabney, *Virginia: The New Dominion* (New York: Doubleday, 1971), 485.
[2] Francis Butler Simkins, "Ku-Klux Klan," *Encyclopedia Americana* (1960), 16, p. 549.
[3] From 1915 to 1979, Virginia forcibly sterilized 7,450 people. Bill Baskervill, Associated Press, on Virginia News Online, 30 Mar 2000. Also, Marian S. Olden, "Sterilization," *Encyclopedia Americana* (1960), 25, p. 629.

These people were different. Urban vacationers who "discovered" the Blue Ridge mountains found the mountaineers to be quaint and amusing, albeit frightening. Their lack of material possessions was evident. Their customs and behaviors were not understood.

Of course, the mountain people were not always models of upright behavior. Many were arrested for moonshining during the Prohibition years of 1920–1933. Alcoholism incited many brawls. Domestic spats sometimes led to murder. Stories of violence on the Blue Ridge made the news, and negative stereotypes were perpetuated. The "do-gooders" of society knew that those unfortunate people needed help. Many were unaware of the strong family loyalties and community ties ensuring that neighbors would look after the welfare of those in need.

However, when the larger society's desire for a public good began to impinge upon the individual rights of this marginal group at the fringe of society, the mountain people were roused from contented resignation to their lot in life. They realized their lack of voice only when their homes and farms were threatened by concerted efforts to create a national park. From hollow to hollow, the incredulous word was passed along, "A park is coming."

Steven T. Mather, the first Director of the National Park Service, was amenable to creating parks in the eastern part of the country where a large population would offer support. In his 1923 annual Report to the Secretary of the Interior he wrote, "There should be a typical section of the Appalachian Range established as a national park with its native flora and fauna conserved and made accessible to public use."[1] In 1924, many sites in the Appalachians were suggested as sites for a national park. The Virginia governor began to see establishing the park in Virginia as a means of promoting the state to its position of pre-Civil War eminence.[2] A group from the Shenandoah Valley thought Massanutten Mountain would be ideal.[3]

> Yosemite and Sequoia National Parks in California were established in 1890. Other parks around western sites of grandeur followed. By an act of Congress in 1916, the National Park Service was established as a bureau of the United States Department of the Interior "to conserve the scenery and the natural and historic objects and the wildlife therein and to provide for the enjoyment of the same in such manner and by such means as will leave them unimpaired for the enjoyment of future generations."
>
> "National Parks and Monuments," *Encyclopedia Americana* (1960) 19, page 740.

---

[1] George Freeman Pollock, *Skyland: the Heart of the Shenandoah Natiional Park* (Chesapeake Book Company, 1960), p. 278.
[2] Darwin Lambert, *The Undying Past of Shenandoah National Park* (Boulder, Col.: Roberts Rinehart, 1989), p. 200.
[3] Pollock, *Skyland*, p. 278.

George Freeman Pollock, 1869–1949, who devoted his life to introducing people to the beauty of the Blue Ridge mountains, had established a rustic guest camp on Stony Mountain near Luray. Known as "Skyland," this resort was host to many prominent families in the eastern cities. Pollock worked feverishly to establish Shenandoah National Park in the Blue Ridge area around Skyland.

In October of 1924, the Northern Virginia Park Association was organized with George Freeman Pollock as president. The object was to "bring about the recommendation of the Blue Ridge area around Skyland as a southern Appalachian national park." Five thousand copies of a brochure entitled "A National Park Near the Nation's Capital" were mailed to members of Congress, Chambers of Commerce, and prominent citizens.[1]

On 12 Dec 1924, the committee adopted the recommendation to form a park in the Blue Ridge between Front Royal and Waynesboro. In the national news, the area was described as seven hundred square miles of "primeval wilderness."[2] (Ambrose and his friends would have laughed derisively as they observed their crops of oats, corn, and wheat and their well-fenced grazing lands.)

The Senate appropriated minimal administrative funds to the Park commission in February of 1925. The 1925 National Conference of State Parks was held at Skyland. Pollock lavishly entertained 250 guests with gourmet food, an orchestra from Washington, and saddle horses for their sightseeing excursions.[3] They liked what they saw.

President Calvin Coolidge signed a bill on 22 May 1926 that authorized both Shenandoah and the Great Smoky to become national parks as soon as the minimum acreages were transferred to the United States. However, according to policy of the National Park Service, no federal funds were available to buy park land.[4] A campaign was mounted in Virginia to raise money to buy land and encourage donations of land.

Soon after Harry F. Byrd became governor early in 1926, the Legislature created the Virginia State Commission on Conservation and Development. Will Carson was named chairman. Carson soon realized that the required 385,000 acres of suitable park land did not exist. A new survey found 327,000 suitable acres. What had been described as a "primeval wilderness" was inhabited by 30,000 people!

---

1 Pollock, *Skyland*, p. 218.
2 Lambert, *Undying Past*, p. 202.
3 Pollock, *Skyland*, p. 229.
4 Lambert, *Undying Past*, p. 203.

The commission didn't waste time in gathering specific information about the land tracts they desired. Inspectors came to Ambrose Shifflett's farm to inventory and appraise all of the buildings, the land, the orchards, and the marketable timber. Summary sheets for each of the three tracts that he owned (where his sister Alice Hansbrough lived) were prepared on 7 Mar 1927. Each summary included Ambrose's remark: "I do not care to sell."[1]

In 1928, when pledges of money had not materialized, the Virginia General Assembly appropriated one million dollars to help buy land for the park.[2] Later that year, Herbert Hoover, who enjoyed fishing for mountain trout, was elected President. Persuaded to establish a fishing camp at the head of the Rapidan, he became a strong advocate of the park. He also became enthused about the dream of a highway on the crest of the mountains, a dream that had been around since 1924. Hoover gave the order to start building the Skyline Drive in 1932.[3]

When Franklin D. Roosevelt was elected president, one of his first New Deal projects was organization of the Civilian Conservation Corps. On 5 Apr 1933, President Roosevelt, by executive order, allotted $10 million to get CCC started. Within a few days, park promoter Carson met with Roosevelt and the president decided to place the first CCC camp in the mountains close to Washington. It opened on May 15. The workers cleared out blight-killed chestnuts and planted thousands of trees, thus landscaping the area close to the Skyline Drive![4]

> The Depression hit Virginia farmers hard. 1930 was one of the worst drought years in history, with rainfall only 60% of normal, crops ruined, and cattle starved. In 1932, Virginia wheat was selling for 50 cents a bushel, the lowest price in 132 years. Virginia's relief program consisted only of putting unemployed to work on the roads,
>
> Virginius Dabney, *Virginia: The New Dominion* (New York: Doubleday, 1971), p. 488.

But Depression realities meant that no more money could be raised to buy park land. Congress reduced the required minimum acreage. The state had passed the Public Park Condemnation Act by which all park tracts in one county could be grouped into one court case. Rockingham County's condemnation proceedings were "pursuant to an order entered the 28th day of June, 1934."

---

1 Shenandoah National Park Archives, State Commission on Conservation and Development Land Records, 1869–1995, Box 69, Folder 54.
2 Lambert, *Undying Past*, pp. 204-210.
3 Lambert, *Undying Past*, pp. 219-220.
4 Lambert, *Undying Past*, pp. 222-223.

MUNIMENTS OF TITLE

of the

STATE COMMISSION ON CONSERVATION AND DEVELOPMENT

(Created an Agency of the Commonwealth of
Virginia by an Act of the General Assembly
of Virginia, approved March 17, 1926,
Acts of 1926, Chapter 169, Page 307.)

in and to

SHENANDOAH NATIONAL PARK LANDS

CONDEMNED

for use as

A PUBLIC PARK AND FOR PUBLIC PARK PURPOSES

In the Condemnation Proceeding
Styled as Follows
The state Commission on Conservation
and Development of the
Virginia Petitioner
v. At Law No. 1829
Cassandra Lawson Atkins and others,
and Fifty-Two Thousand Five Hundred
Sixty-One (52,561) Acres of Land,
more or less in Rockingham County,
Virginia Defendants

Admitted to record the 10th day of August,
1934, pursuant to an order entered the 28th day of
June, 1934, and spread in the Common Law Order Book
No. 20, page 218, in the Clerk's Office of the Circuit
Court of Rockingham County, Virginia.

Rockingham County, Virginia, Deed Book 159, page 1.

Ambrose and the Exodus

The opening page of Rockingham County's Deed Book No. 159 coldly summarizes the legal actions taken. The next few pages in the deed book describe proceedings "under authority of the provisions of Section 14 of the Public Park Condemnation Act" and "The report of the Special Investigators and the Board of Appraisal Commissioners" filed on 2 Aug 1932. The remainder of the volume contains a description of the park land boundaries in Rockingham County, a list of resident and non-resident landowners, and plats of many of the 372 numbered tracts.

By August, all of the deeds were delivered to the Federal government. There were 1,088 tracts involving 196,149 acres in the eight counties. The majority of the tracts deeded were owned by people living outside the park. But, although a few had already decided to move away, 465 families were still living within the park boundary.[1]

In the earliest stages of planning the park, no thought had been given to displacing the human inhabitants of the area. However, given the mood of the times, it is not surprising that federal and state officials had gradually come around to the belief that both the park and the mountain people themselves would benefit if the people moved out.[2]

President and Mrs. Roosevelt helped their cadre of social workers develop plans for resettling the mountain people in "homestead communities." Beginning in September of 1934, communities of small farms were constructed in seven areas just outside the park boundaries.[3] The homestead construction crews salvaged some usable doors and windows from the mountain homes as the inhabitants began to move out. Soon neighbors began helping themselves to supplies or even entire outbuildings. Some families moved into houses that had been evacuated. The CCC workers and park rangers were caught in the middle of confusion, anger, accusations, and misunderstandings.

In November 1934, when Bob Via (who had moved to Hershey, Pennsylvania) brought suit in federal court, claiming that the Virginia land condemnations violated the 14th amendment of the U. S. constitution, there was a last glimmer of hope for the about-to-be displaced persons—and frustration for the protagonists of the park. Via's lawyers argued that the state had "no power to condemn property within the state for the purpose of making a gift of it to the United States." The case was heard at the U.S. District Court at Harrisonburg on 10 Dec 1934. Via lost the case and also lost an appeal on 25 Nov 1935.[4]

---

[1] Lambert, *Undying Past*, p. 241.
[2] Lambert, *Undying Past*, p. 224.
[3] Relatively few of the mountain people chose to "homestead," and others stayed in the subsistence homestead communities for just a short time. Many of the settlement homes were eventually sold to the public. Lambert, *Undying Past*, p. 249.
[4] Lambert, *Undying Past*, p. 237. The latter decision cleared the way for the Shenandoah National Park to be fully established on 26 Dec 1935.

Deeds for the condemned land had been turned over to the United States government in August of 1934, but not all families were satisfied with the terms, the presumed amount of acres, or the price and manner of payment. Some families which had resisted the offer of resettlement still had no idea where they would go when forced to leave their homes.

A few days before being evicted, Ambrose Shifflett dictated a letter of desperation to the President of the United States. His daughter Beulah was chosen to record the plea to President Roosevelt because she had better penmanship. The letter indicates that Am had difficulty convincing the authorities of the total acreage in his farm, and that he, perhaps naively, tried to negotiate a better price for his prime grazing land.

Swift Run, Va.
December 2, 1935

President Roosevelt,
White House,
Washington, D.C.

Dear Mr. Rooosevelt,

My wife and I are writing to you to ask your help in our great trouble. There are three hundred and twenty five acres in my track of land by their own survey. I found it on the park map and they refuse to pay me for it. I bought this land in four different tracts and these were boundage deed and they would not pay me for but one hundred and ninety acres. I wrote to them and they raised it to two hundred acres. But they did not give me any more money per acre. Do you think that this is right or just? Last Friday we were ordered by authorities to be out by December 6.

When we have never taken the money for our land because they would not agree to pay for the acres that were short. Our land is good grazing, good crop and good timber land. We feel this is so unjust and unfair so we have never taken the money that has been offered us by the Park people, hope that we will get justice for our land. It is just impossible for me to get my winter stored crops and stock out by December 6, and find a home to go to. I give them a price but never did get any answer.

I am sixty-four years old and my eyes is bad. I can hardly recognize a distance a woman and a man apart. I more than appreciate if you could save my house if there is any thing you can do. Do it at once for I am here and no place to go. The office told us they were to move us out we ask him where? He said in the road.

You know how dear a home is when it is taken from us and we have no place to go to. We are pleading for help to save our land.

*Yours Truly,
Ambrose W. Shiflett*

It was a polite letter born out of a sense of injustice, anger, frustration, fear, and dread. The letter was received in Washington, stamped by the Department of Interior, and filed.[1]

Somehow, within the next three days, a decision was made that the family would temporarily reside in an old house near Nortonsville that was owned by Ambrose and Laura's oldest son, Dewey. This was the same property in which Laura's father, Burton Morris, had unwisely invested in 1919.[2] Dewey, who lived and worked in Pennsylvania, had acquired the Nortonsville property in 1932. The old house was uninhabited.

Ambrose reported the decision in another letter.

```
                                    5 Dec 1935.
Mr. W. C. Hall
Chairman of the State Conservation and Development
Commission
Richmond, Virginia

Dear Mr. Hall,

   Mr. Hansbrough and I are moving. I have got me a place but I am
asking you could I have some of these old buildings and also Mr.
Hansbrough to for to build some thing for our fowls and stock.
The land owners in the park has been asking for the old buildings
and they gave then to them if they wanted them. And also some of
this old wire to fence up a place to hold my stock. Which the
place I am going to has not got no fence and has no buildings for
fowls and to store away my stock. If you are not the right man
please send it on to the right one. I would more than appreciate
your kindness hope to hear from you soon.

                                    Very truly yours,
                                    Ambrose W. Shifflett[3]
```

---

1 The original letter is lost. My copy of a copy ... of a copy ... was given to me by researcher Barbara Shifflett Hensley of Elkton, Va.
2 See chapter 4, page 60.
3 A typed copy of the letter, on State Commission on Conversation and Development letterhead is in the Park Archives, Box 98, Folder 30.

The same day, someone came from the Simmons Gap mission with an automobile to take Laura, Beulah, 18, Edna, 11, and 6-year-old Kenny off the mountain. Ambrose and 15-year-old Otto stayed behind to tend to the livestock. From Nortonsville the car turned back toward the mountain on the long, bumpy lane which lead to their new home. It was a gray December day when the unhappy family entered the weathered gray house.

Laura built a fire in the fireplace and lighted some kerosene lamps. It was cold and dark and smoky, lonely and dreary in an unfamiliar place. "Pop" was not there. Loud noises from the woods and the distant sound of drunken singing scared mother and children. Recalling the frightening experience, Kenneth said, "We knew we were doomed."

Up on the mountain, Am and Ott spread straw on the floor, and tried to get some rest during that last night in their home. In the morning they fed the livestock, then started driving the cows, sheep, and mules down the long road to Nortonsville—a seven-mile trek. It was Thursday, 6 Dec 1935, the day the "Park people" said they had to be out. The next day a crew came and burned the house they had lived in. The bee hives were destroyed, along with anything else that couldn't be taken. Two old muzzle-loading rifles, forgotten in a bedroom, were gone.

The following Tuesday, Am sent another plea for buildings and wire.[1]

Nortonsville, Va.
December 11, 1935

J. R. Lassiter,
Luray Virginia,

Dear Mr. Lassiter,

I am enclosing to you Mr. Hall letter which I ask him for some of the old buildings and some wire to fence to keep my stock in where I moved to and he refered me to write to you. Where we have moved to we have no place for our fowls and cows. I would be awful thankful if you would help me out in the wire and lumber which the buildings is not much good. please let me hear from you on return mail.

Very Truly Yours,
Ambrose W. Shifflett

---

[1] The pencilled letter to Mr. Lassiter was written on a small tablet.

Two official replies were written to Ambrose the next day.[1] Mr. Lassiter said no.

> United States
> Department of the Interior
> Shenandoah National Park
> Luray, Virginia
>
> December 12, 1935
>
> Mr. Ambrose Shiflett,
>   Nortonsville,
>   Virginia.
>
> Dear sir:
>
>   I am in receipt of your letter of December 11 enclosing Mr. Hall's letter to you in reference to your request for some of the old buildings and fences from your home place in the park.
>
>   I am sorry to inform you that we cannot dispose of any of the property in the park, as the state of Virginia has designated all of the material to be used for subsistence homestead projects, and in accordance with the previous agreement it is necessary that I deny your request.
>
> > Yours very truly,
> > J. R. Lassiter,
> > Engineer in charge

---

[1] Copies of these letters are filed in the Shenandoah National Park Archives, State Commission on Conservation and Development Land Records, 1869–1995, Box 98, Folder 30.

One can almost feel the sigh of relief as the assistant director of the National Park Service dictated a curt reply to the letter Am sent to President Roosevelt.

```
                    United States
              Department of the Interior
                 National Park Service
                     Washington

                                        December 12,1935

Mr. Ambrose W. Shiflett,
     Swift Run, Virginia

Dear Mr. Shiflett:

     By reference from the White House, this Service is
in receipt of your letter of December 2, requesting the
President's aid in securing permissiom to continue to re-
side within the proposed Shenandoah National Park. Since
the receipt of your letter, however, Mr. Wilbur C. Hall,
Chairman of the State Commission on Conservation and De-
velopment, has forwarded to this office a copy of your
letter of December 5 in which you state that you and Mr.
Hansbrough were moving from the area. Therefore, no fur-
ther reply is deemed necessary to your letter of December
2, which has been made a part of our records.

                              Sincerely yours,
                              G. A. Moskey,
                              Assistant Director.
```

The $7,166 that Ambrose received for his 325 acres of good grazing, crop, and timber land had been placed in an escrow account in a Harrisonburg bank. Many months later, when reality overcame indignation, a son took Laura to the bank to withdraw the money.

But in 1935, a new life had to be fashioned. Their temporary home near Nortonsville was larger than the home on the mountain had been. It had a second floor with a stairway at each end of the house. The boys slept in one upstairs room, girls in the other. There was plenty of space, but the chimney would never draw properly. It was always dark and smoky.

Kenneth said, "Mom hated the house, so I did too. As much as possible, I stayed in the kitchen where there were more windows." The family struggled through the winter with cold and sickness.

Am found make-shift materials to house and fence the livestock. In the spring, he planted corn in the red clay soil. The soil was terrible, hard-baked when dry, with knee-deep mud when wet. The occasional automobile attempting to navigate the lane would invariably get stuck in the mud. Laura planted a garden. Perhaps the most memorable gifts of produce were the delicious watermelons.

Since Laura's sister Cissie had moved from the mountain to a small house on adjacent property, she still had that companionship. The children rode the bus to school in Earlysville. There were new friends.

> Milton S. Hershey, 1857–1945, became a successful candy-maker in Lancaster, Pa. In 1903, he returned to the county of his birth and built a factory to manufacture chocolate bars. The prosperity of the business led to the creation of the town of Hershey, the elegant hotel, the amusement park, the sports arena, and the renowned Hershey Industrial School for orphaned boys. Even during the Depression there were jobs at Hershey.

But the family never forgot that this was a temporary stay in a borrowed home. Once again, Am counted on his oldest son, Dewey, to lay out the next steps. Five more of the older children—Pearl, Nettie, Lunzie, Carl and Ed—had settled near Hershey, Pennsylvania. Dewey scouted the area for a place suitable for Pop and Mom. He found a farm for sale near the village of Hanoverdale, three miles west of Hershey.

On 18 Dec 1936, Am and Laura bought a 171-acre property from Benjamin and Mollie Cullers. They paid $2,244.14 in cash and assumed a mortgage of $5,755.66.

> This indenture made the Eighteenth day of December in the year of our Lord one thousand nine hundred and thirty-six (1936), between Benjamin H. Cullers and Mollie B. Cullers, his wife of West Hanover township, Dauphin County and State of Pennsylvania, parties of the first part, and Ambrose W. Shifflet and Laura B. Shifflet his wife of Earlysville, Alvamar county and state of Virginia parties of the second part, Witnesseth, that the said parties of the first part for and in consideration of the sum of Twenty-two hundred forty-four & 14/100 dollars and (subject to a mortgage of $5755.66 which the grantees assume and agree to pay) lawful money of the United States of America, well and truly paid by the said parties of the second part to the said parties of the first part, at and before the sealing and delivery of these presents, the receipt whereof is hereby acknowledged . . .
>
> All that certain tract of land situate in West Hanover Township, Dauphin County, Pennsylvania, bounded and described as follows, to wit: beginning at a hickory tree; thence by land of Levi Miller North sixty-three degrees west twenty-one perches to a post; thence by land of the same south sixty and three quarters degrees west, seventy seven perches to a post; thence by land of same north eighty-six degrees, twenty five perches to

Ambrose and Laura's farm in Pennsylvania, painted by Longenecker in 1980.

a black oak; thence by land of Edward Bell north sixty-three and three quarters degrees west, thirty-four and three tenths perches to a stone; thence by land of A.M. Schaffner north nineteen and one quarter degrees west, one hundred and twentysix perches to a post; thence by land of William Cassel north, sixty-four degrees west three and seven tenths perches to a stone; thence by land of the same north fifteen and one quarter degrees east, forty three perches to a stone; thence by land of John Cassel and a Public road leading from the Union Road to Harrisburg, north eighty seven and three fourths degrees east, one hundred and sixty-six and one tenth perches to a post; thence by land late of Lewis Biever, south thirty and one-half degrees west, twenty-nine and four tenths perches to a stone; thence by land of A.M. Schaffner south thirteen degrees east, thirty-two and nine tenth perches to a stone; thence by lands late of Levi Gingrich Frank Siever and Samuel Bashore; south, one and one-half degrees east one hundred perches to a stone, the place of beginning. Containing one hundred and seventy-one (171) acres more or less.

Being the same premises Wheeler D. Walker, et ux, by deed dated June 6 1922 granted and conveyed to Benjamin H. Cullers and Mary J. Cullers, his wife, (who has since died) said deed being recorded in the Recorder's office of Dauphin County in Deed Book Z Vol. 18 page 297 being the same land sold to Benjamin H. Cullers, by deed from Wheeler D. Walker, widower, dated May 15, 1926 and recorded in Deed Book T, Vol. 21, page 106.

Together with all and singular the tenements . . . subject to a mortgage with interest of $5755.86 given by Benjamin H. Cullers, et ux, to Federal Land Bank of Baltimore, dated Jan. 2, 1934 and recorded at Harrisburg . . . (Mortgage Book U-19-12)

Witnessed by Richard B. Earnest, Justice of the Peace
George D. Shifflett[1]

---

1 Dauphin County, Pa., Deed Book D-24-209, recorded 18 Dec 1936.

Ambrose Shifflett with his mules, Jack, Joe and Hattie. The photo was taken about 1942 at his farm near Hanoverdale, Pennsylvania.

A large brick home graced the farm. Its Pennsylvania German origins were evident in the architecture and in the "summer house" in the rear—a separate building for hot-weather cooking, washing, and other tasks. Although the house had no plumbing, it had been wired for electricity! Kenneth remembered that his mother, while still at Nortonsville, started talking about moving to Pennsylvania, and how they would be able to get light by turning a switch. The thought of electricity in the home was the biggest thing on her mind.

Dewey made arrangements for a big truck to drive to Virginia to move their belongings. Somehow they managed to load all the furniture plus their sheep and mules on the truck. A car came for the family. Leaving the older children with neighbors until the end of the school term, Ambrose, Laura, and Kenneth moved to Pennsylvania on 7 Apr 1937.

Dewey helped Am buy additional stock. Milk from his herd of about 15 cows was cooled in the milk house until picked up daily by trucks from the Hershey chocolate factory. The open fields produced crops of corn, wheat, oats, barley, timothy and alfalfa hay. Am's sons, and sometimes sons-in-law, helped bring in the crops. The large Pennsylvania-type bank barn was filled.

Ambrose W. Shifflett
and
Laura B. (Morris) Shifflett
celebrated their
50th wedding anniversary
with their family on
May 3, 1953.

In 1939, Am purchased an automobile, a Plymouth sedan, for his sons. Am never learned to drive. That same year, a tractor was purchased for the boys to use on the farm. Until he was well into his eighties, Am continued to work hard in the fields with his faithful team of mules. As his muscular strength ebbed, he still enjoyed walking around the farm, often for hours at a time.

Laura planted and gathered from a large vegetable garden. Apples, pears, and peaches were harvested from the orchards. Vines of concord grapes lined the walkway from house to barn. There was plenty to put on the Sunday table for gatherings of the children and grandchildren.

Most of their activity was family centered. At various times, Am and Laura's large home was shared with some of their children's families. The occasional visiting relative from Virginia was impressed by both the dairy farm and a tour through the Hershey chocolate factory. Am and Laura maintained their friendships and contacts with Virginia, but there were new friends from the community who came to visit, to help boil applebutter, or to help with butchering.

In 1947, Ambrose and Laura joined the Hanoverdale Church of the Brethren, although, in line with church practice at that time, this required shaving the mustache which was an integral part of Am's adult identity.

Ambrose and the Exodus

Ambrose and Laura boiled applebutter with the help of family and friends in 1965.

Both Am and Laura lived into their nineties. Although Am had had serious problems with anemia when he was in his 60s, a second wind improved his health. After emergency prostate surgery, Am died on 14 Oct 1967. He was 95. Or was it just 93? Laura lived on with declining stamina and comfort. Pnuemonia took her on 15 Dec 1973. They were buried in the Hanoverdale Church of the Brethren cemetery.

Ambrose and Laura had lived in Pennsylvania for more than 30 years after their forced emigration from the Blue Ridge. Although Laura was appreciative of the less toilsome life and the electric light which enabled her to see, Am harbored a certain bitterness to the end. He had spent two-thirds of his days and all of his youthful energy working in the mountains of Virginia. Ambrose survived the exodus, but life was never the same.

Ambrose Washington Shifflett
and his wife
Laurs Belle (Morris) Shifflett
were buried in the cemetery
at the
Church of the Brethren
Hanoverdale, Pennsylvania

9 A Place Remembered

As the children of Ambrose and Laura Shifflett moved from the Blue Ridge and became assimilated in a larger society, they adopted the attitudes of that society. Each came to believe that the change in place was the best thing that could have happened to them.

Some were thankful that they no longer lived on the mountain where life and work were so hard. Others were grateful for the educational and career opportunities that enabled wider horizons. It is easy to attribute these benefits to the place you live—or your wisdom in choosing that place. But time does not stand still in the place you were born!

The interactive effects of time and place cannot be separated. We may have the option of changing our place, but never the time. Each of us—past, present or future—lives in the most modern of times. As we embrace modern conveniences and current ideas, it is tempting to judge the past in light of the present.

In 1976, Edna, Beulah, and Ken paused in front of the fireplace as they visited the remains of their old home near Simmons Gap.

Edna, Carl, and Allen Shifflet (son of Ken) examined a retaining wall at the site of Ambrose and Laura's former home on the Blue Ridge.

For the early Shifflet and Morris ancestors in Virginia, their time of arrival in America was a major factor in determining what their place would be. The geographical constraints of that place influenced their knowledge of and reactions to changing times. They thought the way they did because they never had the chance to think otherwise.

Whatever their particular circumstances of time and place, they worked and played, erred and learned, loved and laughed. Now the mountain is quiet. The fields have returned to forest. There are few visible reminders of the vitality of life on the Blue Ridge eighty years ago. There are just fading recollections of a place remembered.

The timeless mountains of the Blue Ridge.

Appendix A: Family Records

The pedigrees in this appendix indicate the ancestors of Ambrose Washington Shifflett [2] and of Laura Belle Morris [3] for which we have enough documentation to make reasonable assumptions. As stated in the Preface to this book, there are not enough surviving primary records to provide proof of all relationships.

There were many illegitimate children born to the nineteenth century mothers; the fathers are unidentified. Although their neighbors may have known what was going on, the validity of 100 to 150-year-old hearsay is highly questionable.

However, I have included the possible paternal ancestors of Ambrose Shifflett. Some researchers in the Blue Ridge area have assumed that he was a son of William "Buck" Shifflett. The marriage license applications of Ambrose's older brother and of his younger brother designated Buck as the father. The marriage license for Ambrose did not specify a father; only Eve's name was listed.

Ambrose told several of his children that, according to Eve, his father was the neighbor Asa S. Baugher.[1] Other children were told that it was Buck Shifflett. No primary documentation enables us to know the true story.

Perhaps more circumstantial evidence points to the probability of Buck being the father. This probability with lack of proof is indicated with an asterisk after each identifying number.

---

1 Asa Baugher had served as Justice of the Peace when Mary Ann (Lawson) Shifflett's farm was sold in 1868. Rockingham County, Va., Deed Book 7-78, recorded 3 Feb 1871.

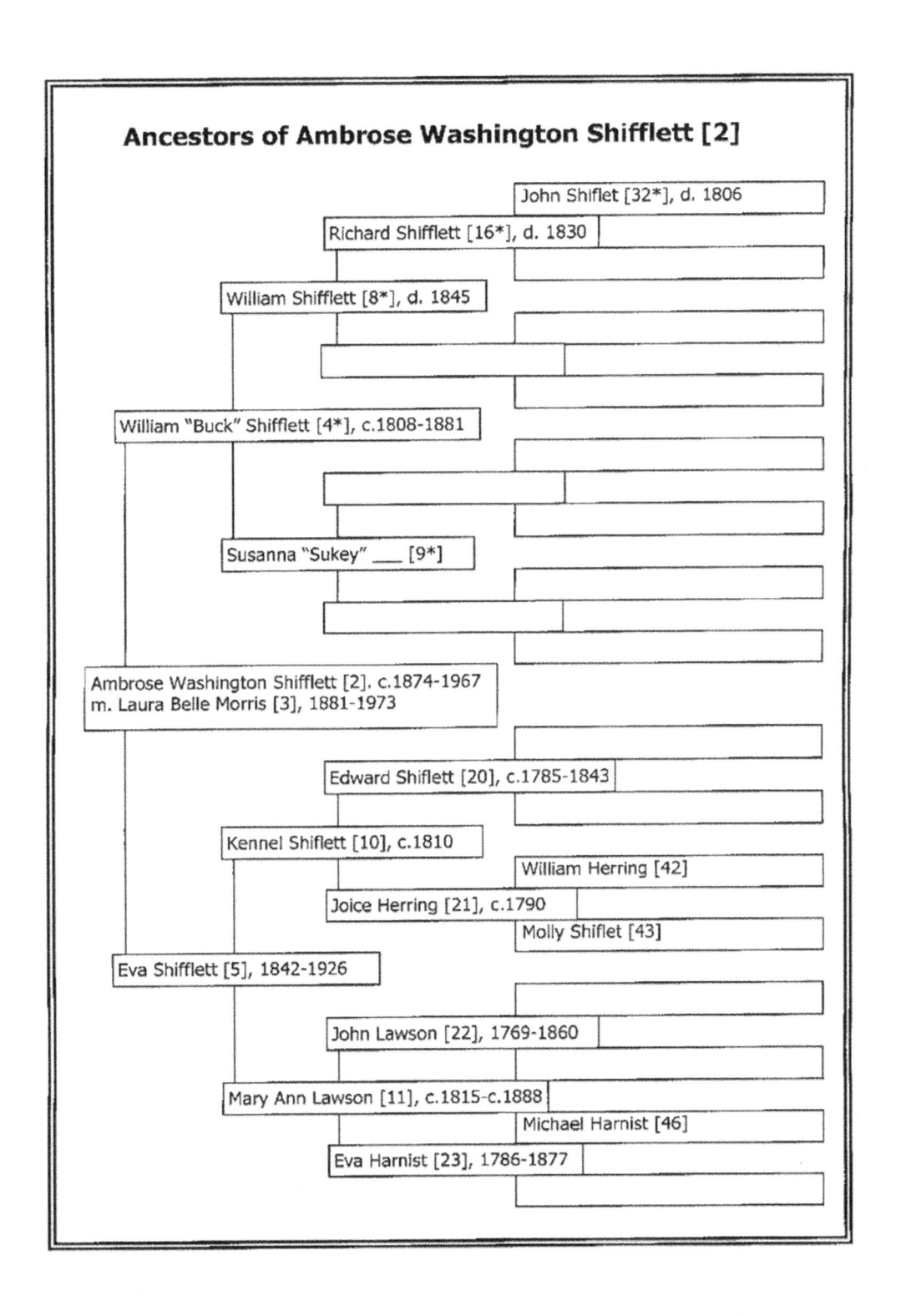

Ancestors of Ambrose Washington Shifflett [2]

- Ambrose Washington Shifflett [2], c.1874-1967
  m. Laura Belle Morris [3], 1881-1973
  - William "Buck" Shifflett [4*], c.1808-1881
    - William Shifflett [8*], d. 1845
      - Richard Shifflett [16*], d. 1830
        - John Shiflet [32*], d. 1806
    - Susanna "Sukey" ___ [9*]
  - Eva Shifflett [5], 1842-1926
    - Kennel Shiflett [10], c.1810
      - Edward Shiflett [20], c.1785-1843
      - Joice Herring [21], c.1790
        - William Herring [42]
        - Molly Shiflet [43]
    - Mary Ann Lawson [11], c.1815-c.1888
      - John Lawson [22], 1769-1860
      - Eva Harnist [23], 1786-1877
        - Michael Harnist [46]

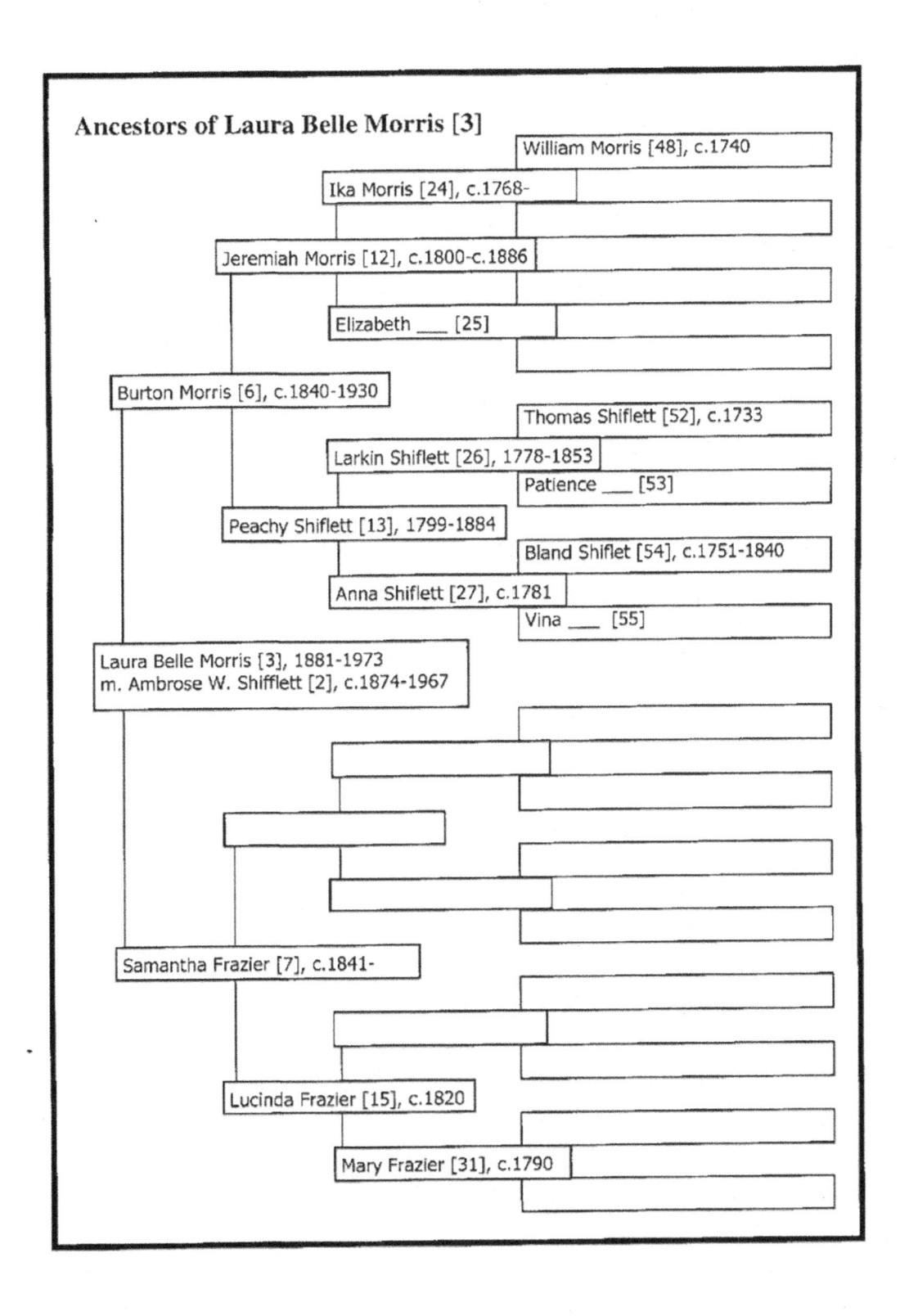

Ancestors of Laura Belle Morris [3]

- William Morris [48], c.1740
  - Ika Morris [24], c.1768-
    - Jeremiah Morris [12], c.1800-c.1886
      - Elizabeth ___ [25]
        - Burton Morris [6], c.1840-1930
          - Thomas Shiflett [52], c.1733
            - Larkin Shiflett [26], 1778-1853
              - Patience ___ [53]
                - Peachy Shiflett [13], 1799-1884
                  - Bland Shiflet [54], c.1751-1840
                    - Anna Shiflett [27], c.1781
                      - Vina ___ [55]

Laura Belle Morris [3], 1881-1973
m. Ambrose W. Shifflett [2], c.1874-1967

- Samantha Frazier [7], c.1841-
  - Lucinda Frazier [15], c.1820
    - Mary Frazier [31], c.1790

Children of Ambrose W. and Laura B. (Morris) Shifflett

1
George Dewey Shifflett
12 Mar 1904–31 Dec 1996
Buried Church of the Brethren Cemetery, Hanoverdale, Pa.
m. Clarise Garrison, 19 Dec 1909–9 Feb 1998
Buried Hummelstown Cemetery, Hummelstown, Pa.

2
Pearl Blanche Shifflett
24 Jan 1906–9 May 2002
Buried Church of the Brethren Cemetery, Hanoverdale, Pa.
m. Jesse Coleman, divorced

3
Nettie Belle Shifflett
15 May 1908-14 May 2006
Buried Hershey Cemetery, Hershey, Pa,
m. Tom Sullivan, 22 Feb 1904–15 Jun 1994
Buried Hershey Cemetery, Hershey, Pa,

4
Ambrose Lunzie Shifflett
15 Nov 1909–5 Sep 1996
Buried Gravel Hill United Methodist Church, Palmyra, Pa.
m. Bertha M. Hetrick, 10 Apr 1914–23 Apr 2002
Buried Gravel Hill United Methodist Church, Palmyra, Pa.

5
Edward Washington Shifflett
17 Apr 1912–22 Nov 2005
Buried Hummelstown Cemetery, Hummelstown, Pa.
m. Mary Frazier, 23 Jul 1916–14 Apr 1967
Buried Hummelstown Cemetery, Hummelstown, Pa.

6
Carl Whitefield Shifflett
3 Jul 1914–27 Dec 1991
Buried Church of the Brethren Cemetery, Hanoverdale, Pa.
m. Beulah E. Hitz, 11 Dec 1919–7 Mar 2001
Buried Gravel Hill United Methodist Church, Palmyra, Pa.

7
Beulah May Shifflett
8 Apr 1917–14 May 2010
Buried Holly Memorial Gardens, Charlottesville, Va.
m. George "Dick" Herring, 9 Jul 1919–7 Nov 2004
Buried Holly Memorial Gardens, Charlottesville, Va.

8
Otto Washington Shifflet
15 Nov 1920–10 Aug 2010
Buried Church of the Brethren Cemetery, Hanoverdale, Pa.
m. Gladys M. Koons, 24 Jun 1924–14 Feb 2005
Buried Church of the Brethren Cemetery, Hanoverdale, Pa.

9
Edna May Shifflet
24 Sep 1923–19 Dec 2012
Buried Church of the Brethren Cemetery, Hanoverdale, Pa.
m. Nicholas Parrell, 19 Sep 1916– 29 Mar 2011
Buried Catholic Cemetery, Middletown, Pa.

10
Kenneth Earl Shifflet
20 Jan 1929–
m. Anne Frysinger, 15 Mar 1933–

Appendix B: Records of the Shenandoah National Park

Records pertaining to the acquisition of Ambrose Shifflett's land for use in the Shenandoah National Park are filed with the State Commission on Conservation and Developments Land Records, 1869–1995, Box 69, Folder 54. They are housed in the Shenandoah National Park Archives near Luray, Virginia.

The following information is from a typed, undated summary of hand-written notes taken during appraisal visits to the property, presumably during 1926. A summary sheet, a printed form with hand-written responses, is dated 27 Mar 1927.

County: Rockingham
District: Stonewall

#178 - Shifflett, Ambrose

Acreage Claimed:	272 A.	Assessed 272	A. Deed 272 A.
Value Claimed:	$10,064	$1,620.00	(1912–26)
			$3,650.00

[Note: A printed claim form with particulars typed in was dated 17 Feb 1931 and signed by A. W. Shifflett. It included the statement: "I claim that the total value of this tract or parcel of land with the improvements thereon is $10,064." No other documents in the file provided an explanation for this amount.]

Area: 325 A.

Location: Hawksbill creek and is entirely within the Park area.

> Note -- It is believed there were errors in the computations of the acreage of the various tracts making up this tract and that Mr. Shifflett owns all the acreage that has been given him.

Incumbrances, counter claims or laps: None known.

Soil: Clay loam of good depth and fertility.

[Note: On a small, undated appraisal sheet, the following comment was penciled: Excellent soil of good depth and fertility on North and Northwest exposure on the larger portion of the tract. The remainder is of average depth and fertility.]

Roads: Nine miles to Elkton over five miles of county road and four miles over Spotswood Trail.

History of tract and condition of timber: The woodland has an estimated stand of 355,000 bd. ft. of saw timber, 40 cords of locust, 2000 cords of extract and 200 cords of pulp wood. A portion of the tract has been heavily cut over.

<u>Timber</u>: 75,000 ft. poplar @ $8.00 per M. $600.00
      240,000 ft. white & red oak @ $4.00 per M   950.00
      40,000 ft. hickory @ $2.00 per M.   80.00
      40 cords locust @ $4.00 per cord   160.00
      1000 cords of extract wood @ .25 per cord   250.00
      200 cords of pulp @ $2.00 per cord   400.00
       $2,450.00

<u>Improvements</u>: Barn: log, 16x49', poor condition - no value.
    <u>Corn house</u>: Log, poor condition - no value.
    <u>Spring house</u>: Frame, 8x15x8', metal roof, fair condition $30.00
    <u>Hen house</u>: Frame, 6x16x6', paper roof, poor condition   15.00
    <u>Pigeon house</u>: Frame, 12x12x8', shingle roof, fair condition   25.00
    <u>Dwelling</u>: Log and frame, 16x33', 5 rooms, porch 8x33', metal roof, stone flues, 3 rooms ceiled, occupied by tenant, spring, solid foundation   600.00
    <u>Barn</u>: Log and frame, 26x45x16', shingle roof, fair condition   350.00
    <u>Old granary</u>: Frame 12x20x10', shingle and metal roof, poor condition   20.00
    <u>Shop</u>: Frame, 12x16x10', paper roof, fair condition   40.00
    <u>Sheep house</u>: (new) Frame, 15x30x12', metal roof, good condition   250.00
    <u>Cow stable</u>: Frame 10x16x10', paper roof, fair condition   <u>35.00</u>
     $1,365.00

[Note: A notation on a summary sheet states that the tenant is Melvin Hansbrough, age 37, resident on tract for 17 years, number in family, 5.]

Value of land by types:

Type	Acreage	Value Per Acre	Total Value
Slope	165	$2.50	$412.50
Cove	90	5.00	450.00
Fg	70	20.00	1,400.00
	325		$2,262.50

Total value of orchard	$ 215.00
Total value of land	2,262.50
Total value of improvements	1365.00
Total value of timber	<u>2,450.00</u>
Total value of tract	$6,292.50
Average value per acre	19.36

Comparison of the Three Parcels in Tract #178

	Parcel 1	Parcel 2	Parcel 3
Rockingham Co. Deed	Book 96-58	Book 132-306	Book 134-174
Purchase date	16 Dec 1912	27 May 1925	27 Jan 1926
Purchased from	H. & F. Eiler	Jesse Wyant	Jesse Wyant
Purchase price	$1,800	$1,600	$250
Total acres*	102 acres on Simmons Gap road, west slope of Main Ridge	150 acres on Simmons Gap road	20 acres on south slope of ridge running west from Main Ridge
Acres cultivated/cleared	25, rolling some rough, some smooth	10 cleared	none
Acres in orchards	2: 95 apple trees, 20 cherry, 100 peach	none	none
Acres in pasture	25, fairly heavy blue grass	none	none
Acres fenced	50, rail, good condition	none	none
Acres cut over within 15 years	none	100, some steep and rough	10, firewood only
Acres in saw timber	50, sloping and fairly smooth	50, some steep and rough, some rolling	10, sloping, some smooth
Timber trees	Chestnut, poplar, Spanish oak	Chestnut, Spanish oak	Chestnut, Spanish oak
Bounded by	N Joseph Wood, Alex Shifflet E Ambrose Shifflett S Charles Davis W Geo. M. Shifflett	N Thomas Yancey E Wm. & E.B. Sellers S H. & F. Eiler W Ambrose Shifflett	N Wm. Sellers E Ambrose Shifflett S Ambrose Shifflett W Joseph Wood

The Ambrose and Laura Shifflett family lived on this property of H. R. and F. D. Eiler. A notation on a summary sheet in Box 65, Folder 20 stated: "Ambrose W. Shifflett resides on tract, age 54, has resided on tract 25 years, number in family, 6."

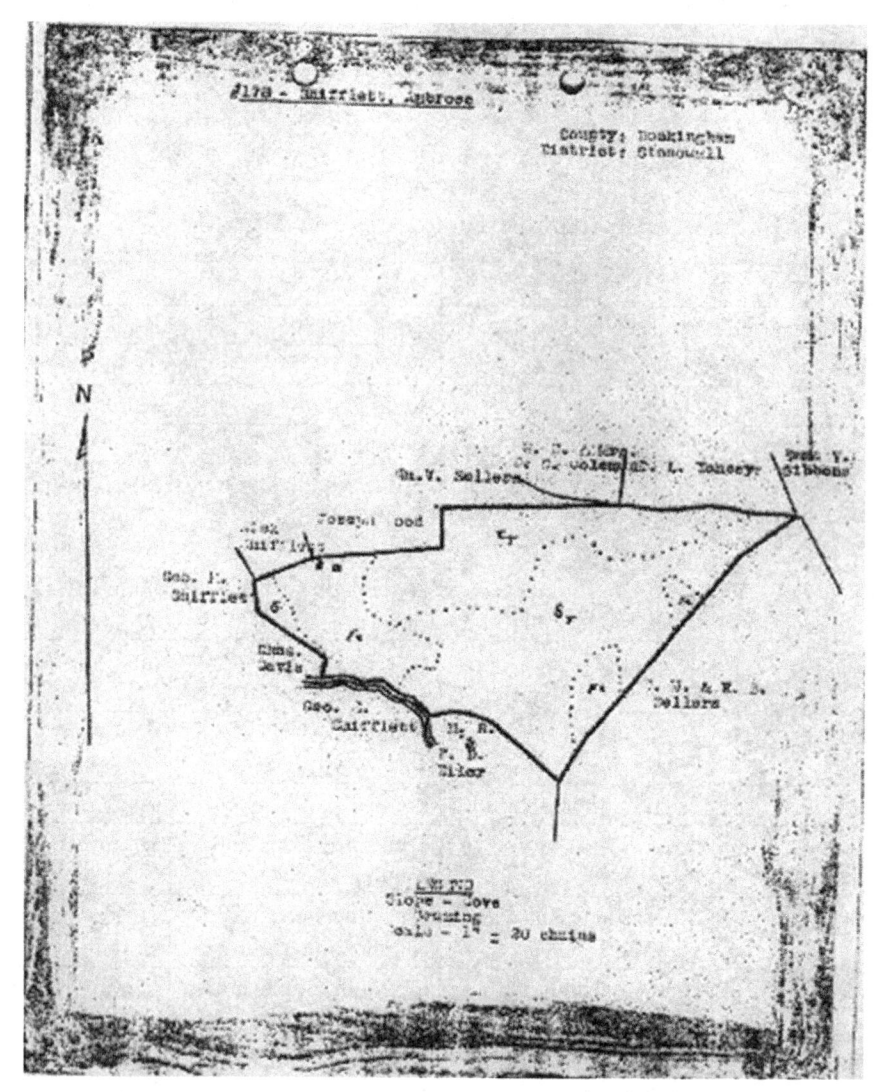

Plat of Ambrose Shifflett's Tract #178, as shown in the Rockingham County, Va., Deed Book 159, page 125.

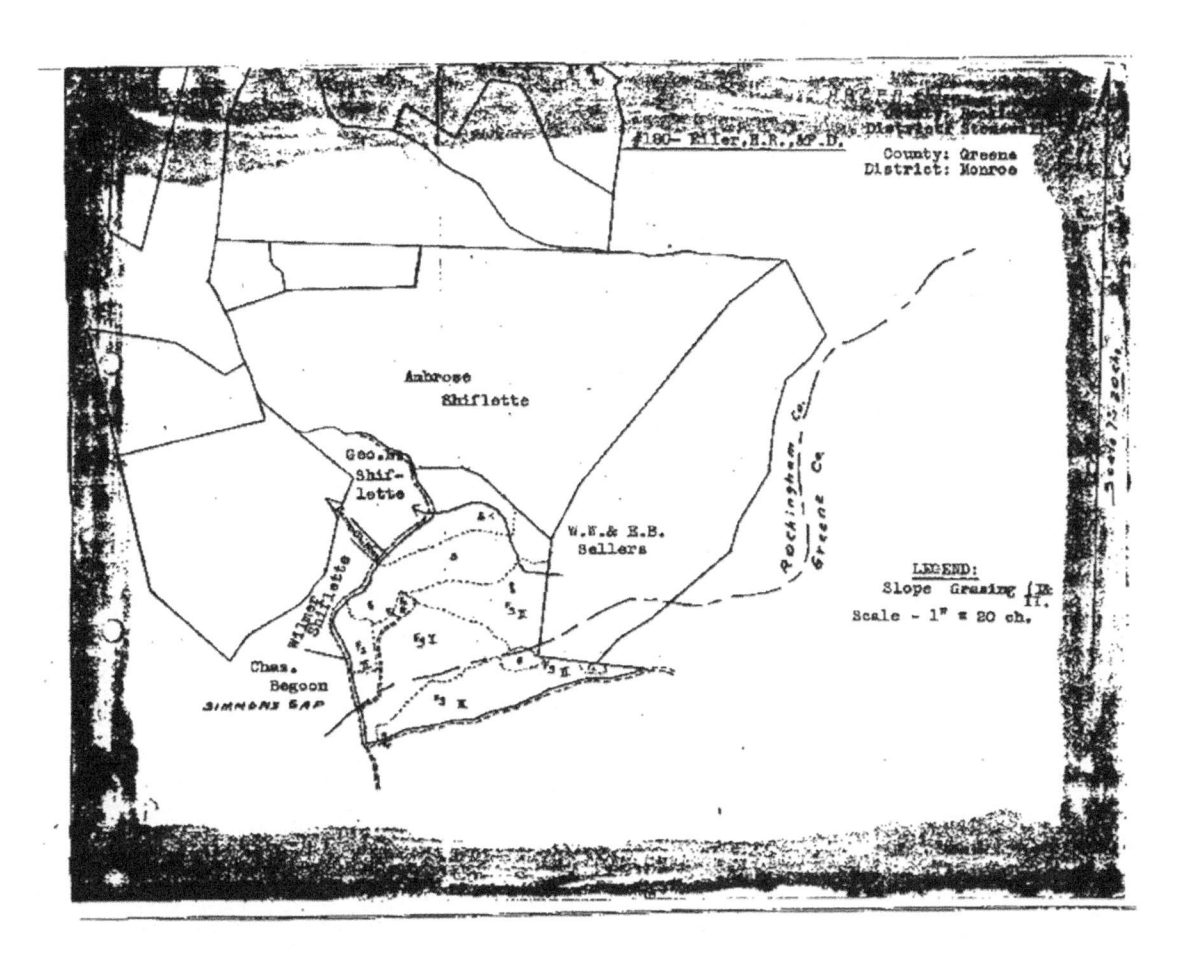

Map of Rockingham County Tract #180 owned by H. R. and F. D. Eiler. Ambrose Shifflett was caretaker and lived on this land from 1902 until evicted by the Shenandoah National Park in December, 1935. The Shifflett home was located about one-half mile from Simmons Gap, just on the Rockingham side of the county line. The map also shows the adjacent tract on the western slope of the mountain that was owned by Ambrose Shifflett.

Tract #180 - Rockingham County, Stonewall District
Tract #157 - Greene County, Monroe District
    Acreage Claimed:165   Assessed: 165 A.   Deed: 165 A.
    Value Claimed:$2,000   Assessed: $2,320.00   Deed: Inherited

<u>Location</u>: Top of Blue Ridge at Simmons Gap, lying in both Rockingham and Greene counties and entirely within the Park area.

<u>Incumbrances, counter claims or laps</u>: None known.

<u>Soil</u>: Sandy loam of good depth and fertility. The wooded portion is very rocky with large cliffs and steep slopes. The first class grazing land has a fine blue grass turf with no weeds or brush and a very little loose rock with moderate slopes. The second class is thin soil with more loose rocks and some outcrops; the slopes are somewhat steep. The Greene County portion has considerable shade on a large portion of it. The soil spews up in the winter and there is sufficient water on the tract.

<u>Roads</u>: Seven miles of good dirt road to Yancey, the nearest shipping point.

<u>History of tract and condition of timber</u>: The tract has been cut over at various times and there has been no fire for several years. On 25 acre of the land there is a good stand of yellow poplar ranging up to 48" DBH with a few other trees. The timber is of good quality. The remainder of the wooded area has a good stand of firewood, and extract wood. The estimate is

45 M. saw timber with 60% of yellow poplar @ $5.00	$225.00
100 cords of extract woood @ 15¢	15.00
300 cords of firewood @ 40¢	120.00
800 locust posts @ 5¢	<u>40.00</u>
	$400.00

<u>Improvements</u>: Tenant house: 14x36', 4 rooms, 1½ story,
2 porches, fair condition $425.00

<u>Barn</u>: Log and frame, 16x37', fair condition	200.00
<u>Spring house</u>: Frame, 8x10', poor condition	5.00
<u>Storage house</u>: Frame, 24x18', shingle roof	75.00
<u>Granary</u>: 10x12', paper roof, good condition	40.00
<u>Corn house</u>: Log, 12x17', paper roof	60.00
<u>Hen house</u>: 8x10'.	<u>30.00</u>
	$835.00

Acreage and value of land by types: (Rockingham County)

Type	Acreage	Value Per Acre	Total Value
Slope	65	$3.50	$ 227.50
Cove	34	42.00	1,428.00
Fg	37	20.00	740.00
Fc	2	40.00	80.00
	138		$2,262.50

Type Acreage Value Per Acre Total Value
Total value of land $2,475.50
Total value of improvements 835.00
Total value of timber 400.00
Total value of orchard 35.00
Total value of tract $3,745.50
Average value per acre 27.14

Acreage and value of land by types: (Greene County)

Type	Acreage	Value Per Acre	Total Value
Slope	3	$2.50	$ 7.50
Cove	10	42.00	420.00
Fg	33	20.00	660.00
Fc	1	40.00	40.00
	47		$1,127.50

Total value of land (Greene County) $1,127.50
Average value per acre 24.00

SUMMARY
Rockingham and Greene Counties

Number of acres in tract: 185
Total value of tract $4,873.00
Average value per acre 26.34

Bibliography of Published Sources

Information about specific Shifflett and Morris families was compiled from wills, deeds, marriage, death, and other records in the Albemarle, Culpeper, Greene, Louisa, Orange, and Rockingham County courthouses. Federal census records enabled calculations of approximate birth years. Full information on these sources is given in the chapter footnotes.

The sources listed below provided historical background and knowledge of Virginia laws and customs.

"Abstracts of Louisa Land Grants," *The Louisa County Historical Magazine*, Vol. 10, No.1 (Summer 1978).

Allen, Henry. "What It Felt Like: Living in the American Century, 1910–1920," *Washington Post*, Tuesday, September 21, 1999.

Alexander, Edward Porter, editor. *Journal of John Fontaine*. Williamsburg: Colonial Williamsburg Foundation, 1972.

Andrews, Matthew Page. *Virginia: The Old Dominion*. New York: Doubleday, Doran & Company, 1938.

Baird, Nancy, and Kate Hatch. *Abstracts of Louisa County, Virginia Will Books, 1743–1801*. Compilers, 1964.

Ballagh, James Curtis. *White Servitude in the Colony of Virginia*. Baltimore: John Hopkins University Studies, 13th Series, No. VI-VII, 1895.

Bean, Bennett R. *The Peopling of Virginia*. Boston: Chapman Co., 1938.

Bruce, Thomas. *Southwest Virginia and Shenandoah Valley*. Richmond, Va.: J. L. Hill, 1891.

Brydon, George MacLaren. *Religious Life of Virginia in the Seventeenth Century*. Williamsburg, Va.: The Virginia 350th Anniversary Celebration Corporation, 1957.

Church and Family Cemeteries of Rockingham County–East of Route 11. Copied by the Massanutten Chapter of the Daughters of the American Revolution, 1965–1971.

Cocke, Charles Frances. *Parish Lines, Diocese of Virginia.* Richmond, Va.: Virginia State Library, 1967.

Coldham, Peter Wilson. *Bonded Passengers to America: Vol.1, History of Transportation, 1615–1775.* Baltimore: Genealogical Publishing Company, 1983.

Crozier, William A., editor. *Spotsylvania County Records, 1721–1800: Transcriptions from the Original Files at the County Court House.* Baltimore: Southern Book Co.,1955.

Dabney, Virginius. *Virginia: The New Dominion.* New York: Doubleday, 1971.

Davidson, Dexter Ralph. "Frederick W. Neve, Mountain Mission Education in Virginia, 1888–1948." Ph.D. Thesis, University of Virginia, 1982.

Davis, Rosalie Edith, abstractor. *Fredericksville Parish Vestry Book, Indentures and Processioning Returns, 1742–1787.* Volume 2.

Davis, Rosalie Edith. "Fredericksville Parish –The EarlyYears." *The Louisa County Historical Magazine*, Vol. 13, Number 2 (Winter, 1981–1982).

Dorman, John Frederick, abstractor and compiler. *Orange County, Virginia Will Book 2, 1744–1778.* Washington, D.C.: compiler, 1961.

Dowdey, Clifford. *The Virginia Dynasties.* Boston: Little, Brown and Company, 1969.

Doyle, James W., Jr., "Saint Stephen's Parish, King and Queen County, James Madison and the Bill of Rights," *Tidewater Virginia Families*, Vol. 5, No.1.

Doyle, James W., Jr. "The Mayflower Comes to Virginia, 1633," *Tidewater Virginia Families,* Vol. 3, No. 4.

Dudley, Lavinia O., editor-in-chief, *Encyclopedia Americana.* New York: Americana Corporation, 1960.

Estes, Earl W., transcriber, *Greene County, Virginia, Graveyard Survey*, conducted 1995–1998. Greene County Historical Society, 1999.

Fishbach, Marshal W. *The Virginia Tradition.* Washington, D.C.: Public Affairs Press, 1956.

Fischer, David Hackett. *Albion's Seed: Four British Folkways in America.* New York: Oxford University Press, 1989.

Garraty, John A. and Mark C. Carnes, editors. *American National Biography.* New York: Oxford University Press, 1999.

Grundset, Eric G. *Historical Boundary Atlas of the Potomac, Shenandoah, and Rappahannock Valleys of Virginia and West Virginia.* Fairfax, Va.: Author, 1999.

Heads of Families, Virginia: Records of the State Enumerations, 1782–1785. Washington, D.C.: Government Printing Office, 1908.

Genealogies of Virginia Families, 5 volumes. Baltimore: Genealogical Publishing Co., 1981.

Hening, William Walter. *The Statutes at Large: being a Collection of all the Laws of Virginia.* 13 volumes. 1823. Reprint, Charlottesville, Va.: University Press of Virginia, 1969.

Herring, Beulah Shifflett. *Mountain Memories and Growing Up in the Blue Ridge.* Typescript, February, 1990.

Isaac, Rhys. *The Transformation of Virginia, 1740–1790.* New York: W. W. Norton, 1982.

Keezel, Mary Nicholas. *Rescuing the Court Records.* Pamphlet of the Rockingham County Historical Society, 1970.

Kneebone, John T. et al. *Dictionary of Virginia Biography.* Vol. 1. Richmond, Va.: The Library of Virginia, 1998.

Kocher, A. Lawrence and Howard Dearstyne. *Shadows in Silver: A Record of Virginia, 1850–1890.* New York: Scribner's Sons, 1954.

Lambert, Darwin. *The Undying Past of Shenandoah National Park.* Boulder, Co.: Roberts Rinehart, 1989.

Lederer, John. *The Discoveries of John Lederer.* Translated by Sir William Talbot. London: Heyrick, 1672. Special Collections Library, University of Virginia Library.

Little, Barbara Vines, compiler. *Orange County Tithables, 1734–1782.* Compiler, 1988.

MacMaster, Richard K. *Augusta County History, 1865–1950.* Staunton, Va.: Augusta County Historical Society, 1987.

Mansfield, James Roger. *A History of Early Spotsylvania.* Orange, Va.: Green Publishers, 1977.

Miller, Ann L. *Antebellum Orange.* Orange, Va.: Orange County Historical Society, 1988.

Moger, Allen W. "The Rebuilding of the Old Dominion, a Study in Economics, Social and Political Transition from 1880–1902." Ph.D. dissertation, Columbia University, 1940.

Neve, Frederick W. *Light in Dark Places.* Ivy Depot, Va., 1905. Albert H. Small Special Collections Library, University of Virginia Library.

Nugent, Nell Marion, abstracter. *Cavaliers and Pioneers: Abstracts of Virginia Land Patents and Grants,* Vol. II, 1666–1695. Richmond: Virginia State Library, 1977.

Nugent, Nell Marion, abstracter. *Cavaliers and Pioneers: Abstracts of Virginia Land Patents and Grants,* Vol. III, 1695–1732. Richmond: Virginia State Library, 1979.

Perkins, Kathleen R. "Abstracts of Law Order Books 1742–1748." *The Louisa County Historical Magazine*, Volumes 9-13.

Pollock, George Freeman. *Skyland: the Heart of the Shenandoah National Park.* Chesapeake Book Company, 1960.

Powell, Eugene D. *The 1860 Federal Census, Greene County, Virginia.* Quinque, Va.: Compiler, 1998.

Powell, Eugene D. *Marriage Records of Greene County, Virginia, 1838–1900.* Quinque, Va.: Compiler, 1998.

Price, Jacob M. "The Rise of Glasgow in the Chesapeake Tobacco Trade, 1707–1775." *William and Mary Quarterly,* 3rd series, XI (April 1954).

Reaney, P. H. and R. M. Wilson. *A Dictionary of English Surnames.* Third edition. London: Routledge, 1991.

Reeder, Carolyn and Jack. Shenandoah Heritage, *The Story of the People Before the Park.* Washington, D.C.: Potomac Appalachian Trail Club, 1978.

1850 Rockingham County, Virginia, Free Population Census, Slave Census, Mortality Schedule, Social Statistics. Transcribed by the Harrisonburg-Rockingham Historical Society. Athens, Ga.: Iberian Publishing Co., 1997.

Salmon, Emily J., and Edward D.C. Campbell, editors. T*he Hornbook of Virginia History.* Fourth edition. Richmond, Va.: Library of Virginia, 1994.

Scott, W. W. *A History of Orange County, Virginia: From it's Formation in 1734 (O.S.) to the end of Reconstruction in 1870; compiled mainly from Original Records.* Richmond: Everett Waddy Co., 1907.

Shifflett, L. F. and Barbara Shifflett Hensley, compilers and editors. *Shiflet (and variant spellings) 1700-1900.* Compilers, 1995.

Shifflett, L. F. and Barbara Shifflett Hensley, compilers and editors. *Shifflet vs. Shifflett: A Greene County, Virginia, Chancery Cause, 1860–1879.* Compilers, 1996.

Sullivan, Nettie Shifflett. *Mountain Memories.* Typescript, undated.

Torrence, William Clayton. *Virginia Wills and Administrations, 1632–1800.* 1930. Reprint, Baltimore: Genealogical Publishing Co., 1981.

Virginia Military Records from The Virginia Magazine of History and Biography, the William and Mary College Quarterly, and Tyler's Quarterly. Baltimore: Genealogical Publishing, 1983.

Tyler, Lyon Gardiner, editor. *Encyclopedia of Virginia Biography*. New York: Lewis Historical Publishing, 1915.

Vogt, John, and T. William Kethley, Jr. *Albemarle County Marriages, 1780–1853*. 3 volumes. Athens, Ga.: Iberian Publishing Company, 1991.

Vogt, John, and T. William Kethley, Jr. *Orange County Marriages, 1747–1850*. Revised edition. Athens, Ga.: Iberian Publishing Company, 1990.

Vogt, John, and T. William Kethley, Jr. *Rockingham County Marriages, 1778–1850*. Athens, Ga.: Iberian Publishing Company, 1984.

Ward, Roger G., abstractor. 1*815 Directory of Virginia Landowners (and Gazeteer)*: Volume 4: Northern Region. Athens, Ga.: Iberian Publishing Company, 1999.

Ward, Roger G., abstractor. *1815 Directory of Virginia Landowners (and Gazeteer)*: Volume 1: Central Region. Athens, Ga.: Iberian Publishing Company, 1997.

Wayland, John W. *A History of Rockingham County, Virginia*. Harrisonburg: C. J. Carrier, 1972.

Weisiger, Benjamin B., III. *Albemarle County, Virginia, Court Papers 1744–1783*. Richmond: Compiler, 1987.

Wertenbaker, Thomas J. *The Planters of Colonial Virginia*. 1922. Reprint, Baltimore: Genealogical Publishing Company, 1997.

Wingfield, Marshall. *A History of Caroline County, Virginia*. 1924. Reprint, Baltimore: Genealogical Publishing Co., 1969.

Wood, Gordon S. *The Radicalism of the American Revolution*. New York: Vintage Books, 1993.

Index of Names

All of the variant spellings for the major surnames have been listed as a single entry. For example, all of the Shiflet, Shifflet, Shiflett, Shifflett, and Shifflette surnames are indexed under SHIFLET, no matter how the name was spelled in any particular document. Women are listed under their maiden names and all married names, with the maiden names indicated in parentheses when known. A range of numbers indicates the primary story of that individual.

The pedigree numbers in square brackets are specific to the direct ancestors on the Ambrose Shifflett family tree. However, within each surname section, the numbers clarify relationships and help to keep the generations in perspective. Each father's number is twice that of his child; the mother's number is twice plus one (e.g., Eva Shifflett [5], Kennel Shifflett [10], Mary Ann Lawson [11]. In a few instances, an asterisk within the bracket, e.g., [86*], indicates a probable ancestor for which there is not sufficient evidence for proof.

Names in footnotes and other sources notes are included only if the individual was a contemporary or relative of the ancestor.

Index

A

Abbot
William B. 69
Abbott
William B. 81
Alexander
Eaton 89
Rebecca Frances (Shifflett) 89
Allen
Abraham 20

Alves
George 12, 41
Andrew
Jacob 87
Peggy 87
Austin
Henry 44

B

Barbour
Thomas 44
Bartlett
John 73
Joseph 69
Bashore
Samuel 128

Baugher
Asa S. 86
George 70, 71
Joseph 97
Rebecca 75
Samuel 69
Baylor
John 17
Beery
Elizabeth Margaret 88
George 88
Sally 88
Bell
Edward 127
Biever
Lewis 128

Biggs
  C. H. 63
Billings
  Luther 69
Bingham
  George 31, 32, 33, 38, 48
Bruce
  Loudon B. 38
  Vina (Shiflet) 38
Bryan
  Jeremiah 23, 42
Burke
  R. M. 104
Byrd
  Harry F. 118

C

Cabot
  John 2
Carson
  Will 118
Cartier
  Jacques 2
Cassel
  John 128
  William 128
Catterton 59
  Michael 35
Chapman
  James 37
  Richard 44
  William 52
Coleman
  Daniel 17, 18
  Delia (Lawson) 77
  William 77
  W. W. 104, 105
Collier
  Chapman 88
  Columbia 88
  Lottie 88
Collins
  Elizabeth 14
Columbus
  Christopher 2
Comstock
  Miss 111
Conrad
  Henry 70
Cook
  Henry 52, 54
Coolidge
  Calvin 118
Coursey
  William 20
Crawford
  Matilda 90
  Matilda (Shifflet) 87
  Obadiah 103
  Sarah 53
  Sidney 55
  Wm. Nevel 87, 90
Creed
  Matthew 42
Cullers
  Benjamin H. 127
  Mary J. "Mollie" 127, 128

D

Dabney
  George 41
Davis
  Charles 72, 87–93, 98, 102
  Isaac 44
  Jackson 77
  Jane (Shifflett) 89
  John 12, 18, 45
  Julia (Lawson) 77
  Lewis 44, 45, 49
  Mary 12, 89
  Susanna 34
Dickenson
  John 20
Dunkler
  M. A. 84
Dunn
  T. M. 60
  William G. 84

E

Earnest
  Richard B. 128
Eaton
  Alexander 90
  Benjamin 89
  Gilly 89
  Rebecca Frances 90
  Thomas 88
  William 54
Eiler
  Fox D. 98
  Howard F. 101
  Howard R. 98
Ellett
  Gilbert 14
Elliot
  Parrotte 36
Ergentright
  George 44
Esty
  Sinnes 84

F

Farish
  Robert 17, 18
Franklin
  Virginia 87
Fraser
  John 17

Index

Frazer
 Dunkliant 18
Frazier
 Alexander 20
 Eliza (Lawson) 77
 Henry 77
 John 20
 Lucinda [15] 55
 Samantha [7] 55
 Shadrack 48

G

Gambill
 Matthew 72
Garrett
 Polly 36
Garver
 David 74
 Rebecca 74
Geer
 Elizabeth 47
Gentry
 C. E. 60
Gibson
 John 38, 39, 76
Gilmore
 David 85, 86
Gingrich
 Levi 128
Goodall
 Isaac 75

H

Hall
 Samuel 59
 Victoria 59
 W. C. 123, 124
Ham
 Lucy 50

Hansbrough
 Alice (Shifflett) 92, 119
 Jordan 95
 Melvin 92, 95, 123
 Roy 92
 Sarah 95
Harnist
 Eva [23] 67
 Johannes 67
 John 67
 Michael 67
Harris
 H. F. 60
Herren
 William 23
Herring
 Beulah (Shifflet) 133
 Caroline 85
 Edmund 18
 Edward 18
 George 72, 74, 85, 86, 89
 James 31
 James R. 79
 Joice [21] 29, 32, 79
 Loudon 74
 Lucinda 31
 Margaret 86
 Mary 74
 Molly (Shiflet) [43] 79
 Nancy (Lawson) 72
 Nicholas 72
 Polly 74
 William 31
 William [42] 29, 79
Hershey
 Milton S. 127
Holley
 Amanda (Lawson) 77
 Samuel 77
Holman
 J. K. 60

Hoover
 Herbert 119
Hunter
 David 69
Hupp
 Jacob 76
 Matilda 70, 71
 Matilda (Lawson) 76
Huston
 Huston 55
 Killis 55

K

Keezel
 Mary 69
Knight
 Henry 101
Kyger
 Doctor 103

L

Lamb
 Betty 34
 Richard 34
Lassiter
 J. R. 124, 125
Lawson
 Albert 77
 Alfred 74, 75
 Amanda 77
 Caroline (Herring) 77, 85
 Delia 77
 Eliza 77
 Elizabeth 75
 Eva (Harnist) [23] 67–78, 85
 Frances (Lawson) 75
 John 77
 John [22] 67–78, 80, 81, 85
 Joseph 72, 75
 Julia 77

Lucinda 74
Malinda 76
Marcus 74
Margaret Caroline 73
Mary Ann [11] 76, 80–96
Moses 70, 74, 75
Nancy 32
Selena (Snow) 75
Theophilus 70, 71, 72, 73, 77, 85, 86

Lederer
John 11

Lord Delaware 3

M

Madison
Ambrose 48
John 17, 18
Marchant
Miss 111
Marsh
William 54
Marshall 71
Malinda (Lawson) 71, 76
William 70, 71, 76
May
John 17, 18
McGahey
Tobias 70
Miller
Levi 127
Mooney
Thornton 36
Morris
Ann 27, 48
Ann (Shiflet) 30
Artamis (Shiflett) 52, 54
Barbara Ellen 56–57, 60, 63
Burton [6] 52, 55–66, 94, 99
Caroline 64

Cecelia "Cissie" 57, 64, 107, 127
Daniel S, 62
David 47
Elijah 44, 45, 47
Elizabeth ____ [25] 46–50
Elizabeth (Geer) 47
Ella J. 57, 63
Emanuel 60
Emily J. 57, 63
Fannie (Sowers) 55
Frances (Crawford) 62
George E. 57, 63
Hustin 52
Ichabod 49
Ika [24] 44–49
James 44, 47, 49, 50
Jane (Shiflett) 54
Jeremiah [12] 49–54
John 49
John "Bev" 62
John S. 56–57
Killis 52
Laura [3] 94
Laura B. [3] 58, 63
Manuel 64
Mary 42
Mary Frances 56–57, 62
Mathias 47
Matthew 44
Paschal 50
Patsy (Shiflett) 47
Peachy (Shifflet) [13] 51–54
Peachy (Shiflet) [13] 38
Polly 48
Rias 60, 63
Richard 27, 30, 32, 38, 39, 48, 52, 55
Sally 50
Samantha (Frazier) [7] 55–66, 99

Samuel 41
Sarah Catherine 56, 62
Smith 64
Sowers 52, 54
Susanna 50
Sylvanus 41
Thomas 27, 30, 32, 38, 39, 41
William 13, 20, 23, 27, 28, 30, 32, 38, 39, 41–42, 44, 16, 46
William [48] 44–48
Moskey
G. A. 126

N

Neve
Frederick W. 108

P

Parrell
Edna (Shifflet) 133
Parrott
Charles 79
Pigg
John 18
Plecker
Walter A. 116
Pocahontas 4
Pollock
George Freeman 118
Powell
Honorarius 23
Honorias 42
James 23
Jeremiah 54
Jerry 103

R

Raleigh
Sir Walter 2

Index

Randolph
  Thomas M. 35
Roach
  Killis 63, 64, 94, 95, 101
Rodgers
  William 38
Rolfe 4
  John 4
Roosevelt
  Eleanor 121
  Franklin D. 119, 121
Rose
  Samuel 20

S

Schaffner
  A. M. 128
Sellers
  Dr. 54
  William 103
  W. W. 105
Shiflet
  Absalom 32, 79
  Adam Linneaus 39
  Ahas 62
  Alex 104
  Alice 92
  Allen 134
  Ambrose [2] 92–96
  Ambrose W. [2] 60, 61, 63, 97–114, 115–132
  Ann 30
  Anna [27] 31, 34, 35–38
  Benson 34
  Betty (Lamb) 34
  Beulah 61, 103, 124
  Blan 29
  Bland 31
  Bland [54] 30, 33
  Cally 39

  Carl 103, 127, 134
  Cathy 31
  Charles E. 94
  Columbia (Collier) 88
  Davis 94
  Dewey 61, 103, 127–128
  Dorothy 92
  Early 31
  Edna 103, 111, 124
  Edward 127
  Edward [20] 29, 79, 84
  Edwin 103
  Elizabeth 27, 31, 32, 34, 36, 38
  Elizabeth (Lamb) 34
  Elizabeth Margaret (Beery) 88
  Elizabeth (Powell) 28
  Elizabeth (Snow) 34
  Emily 31
  Emma 94
  Eva "Eve" [5] 85, 88, 90–96, 97
  Fielding 38
  Francis 85
  George D 128
  Giney 31
  Hastin 52
  Henderson 31, 39
  Henry 36, 85
  Henry White 79, 88, 90
  Hosea 102
  James 32, 36, 52
  Jane 85
  John 14, 20, 27, 28, 29, 34
  John S. B. 31
  Joice (Herring) [21] 79
  Joice (Powell) 28
  Jonas 94
  Kennel [10] 76, 80–87

  Kenneth 103, 124, 133
  Larkin [26] 31, 34, 35–38, 51
  Larry 94
  Laura B. (Morris) [3] 94, 99–114, 115–132
  Lillie F. 94
  Lucretia 52
  Lunzie 103
  Lydia 54
  Margaret E. 90
  Martha 94
  Mary 54, 85
  Mary A. 72
  Mary Ann (Lawson) [11] 71, 76, 80–96, 97
  Mary E. 88, 90
  Mary (Powell) 33
  Matilda 36, 39, 85, 87
  Mattie E. 94
  May Bell 94
  Mildred 32
  Mildred (Herrin) 32
  Milley 39
  Molly [43] 29
  Nancy 32
  Nancy (Lawson) 76
  Nathaniel 29
  Nelson 79–80
  Nettie 103, 127
  Nicholas 70, 76
  Noah 86
  Noah Clark 87, 89
  Otis 92
  Otto 61, 103, 124
  Overstreet 38
  Overton 31
  Patience ___ [53] 28, 33–34
  Patsy 47
  Peachy [13] 38, 51
  Pearl 60, 103, 127

Pleasant 33
Polly 31
Rachel J. 89
Rebecca Frances 89
Rhoda 31
Rias 61
Richard 28, 34
Richard [16*] 29
Russell 94
Sarah 27, 30
Sarah Catherine (Morris) 62
Sarah (Herring) 31
Scott 85
Slaten 50
Stephen 14, 28
Stephen Palmer 31
Steven 23
Susan 94
Susanna (Davis) 34
Susannah 30
Susanna (Morris) 50
Theophilus 88
Thomas 34
Thomas [52] 28, 33–34
Vina 32, 38
Virginia (Franklin) 87
William 23, 27, 52
William [8*] 29
William [86] 29
William J 92
Winny (Herring) 32
Winston 32

Shiplet
Edward 80
Nelson 80

Shover
W. S. 58

Siever
Frank 128

Sims
James 35

Sislett
Steven 12

Sistlett
John 18
Stephen 18

Slaughter
George 14

Smith
Joseph 60

Snow
Elizabeth 34
James 75
Molly 34
Selina 75
Thomas 34, 44

T

Taylor
George 48
Hubbard 48
James 12, 42, 48, 49

Tazewell
Littleton W. 80

Thomas
Jacob 87

V

Via
Bob 121

Vie
C. E. 60

W

Walker
Wheeler D. 128

Webster
E. W. 58

White
Jeremiah 27

Willory
Abraham 13

Wingfield
W. L. 95

Wood
Joseph 102, 105
Mary 89
Mary A. 71, 72, 86

Woods
John D. 86

Woodward
James 41

Wyant
David 75, 76
Elizabeth 72
Elizabeth (Lawson) 75
Frances 74
Isaac 70
Jesse 89, 102, 103, 104, 105
Lucy 98, 101
Martha J. 103, 105
R. F. 98, 101
Wm. H. 105

Wyatt
Joseph 12

Y

Yancey
T. L. 103, 105

*****

Made in the USA
Middletown, DE
16 March 2023